Case Studies
for Inclusive Schools

Case Studies
for Inclusive Schools

Peggy L. Anderson

pro·ed
An International Publisher

8700 Shoal Creek Boulevard
Austin, Texas 78757-6897

© 1997 by PRO-ED, Inc.
8700 Shoal Creek Boulevard
Austin, Texas 78757-6897

Library of Congress Cataloging-in-Publication Data

Anderson, Peggy L.
    Case studies for inclusive schools / Peggy L. Anderson.
        p.   cm.
    Includes bibliographical references and index.
    ISBN 0-89079-703-X (softcover : alk. paper)
    1. Mainstreaming in education—United States—Case studies.
  2. Handicapped children—Education—United States—Case studies.
  I. Title.
LC4031.A65   1997   96-34143
371.9'046—dc20   CIP

This book is designed in Goudy and Frutiger.

Production Manager: Alan Grimes
Production Coordinator: Karen Swain
Managing Editor: Tracy Sergo
Art Director: Thomas Barkley
Reprints Buyer: Alicia Woods
Editor: Tama M. Montgomery
Editorial Assistant: Claudette Landry
Editorial Assistant: Suzi Hunn
Cover illustration by Alexandra Kazmierski, Willow Creek Elementary School, Englewood, CO.

Printed in the United States of America

3 4 5 6 7 8 9 10   01 00 99

To my students, who are my teachers.

Contents

Chapter One
Academic and Language Needs   1

Chapter Two
Cognitive and Adaptive Needs   31

Chapter Three

Attentional Needs   63

Chapter Four

Affective Needs   85

Chapter Five

Physical Needs   115

——— Chapter Six ———

Communication Needs 149

——— Chapter Seven ———

Pervasive Developmental Needs 171

——— Chapter Eight ———

Sensory Needs 191

——— Chapter Nine ———

Gifted and Talented Needs 219

Preface

Case Studies for Inclusive Schools was written to provide teacher education students with a stimulating format for understanding a variety of inclusion issues in the schools. Throughout my career I have come to the understanding that my students learn best and enjoy learning most when they are taught through the use of case studies, or "stories." On innumerable occasions, I have watched a sea of glazed expressions turn to heightened interest, and I have listened to the inevitable hush that descends upon the classroom as I begin a retelling of the experiences that I have encountered in my 20-year career in the field. My case studies have allowed me to give life to my teaching. Through the years, I began to write down these stories I have observed and put them into different formats for group projects, exam questions, and portfolio artifacts. Student response has always been overwhelmingly positive. It appears my students are fascinated by the problems that occur in real-life situations—and they certainly appear to be much more interested in this content than in their textbooks. I have exploited this interest by making these case studies an integral part of all the classes that I teach. It is my distinct impression that since modifying my courses in this manner, my students not only are much more receptive learners, but they also retain information better because they can relate it to specific experiences.

This book focuses on problem solving from a collaborative perspective. It is my sincere belief that students with disabilities are best served when concerned parties work together to provide them with the most appropriate education possible. Families, teachers, and administrators need to join together to establish a support system that enables a child with disabilities to fulfill his or her potential. This book does *not* attempt to make any recommendations regarding the best instructional method, placement, or any other course of action with regard to solving specific problems. It was written to encourage teacher education students to explore the different attitudes, problems, and situations that arise in the schools.

The cases that were included in this book were not intended to be representative of the multitude of different inclusion issues that exist for all children with disabilities. It was meant to provide a sampling of problems associated with integrating students with disabilities into the public school system. As my colleagues read my work, many commented that I needed to add a case regarding another type of child, school, teacher, or parent. If I had agreed to do so, I would still be writing. Because of the individual differences in children, parents, teachers, and administrators, it would be impossible to develop a compendium of cases covering all the challenges of inclusion in the schools. I stopped at 70 case studies, but I am well aware of my colleagues' advice—there could be twice as many stories in this book, and I still would not have been able to provide more than a sampling of the problems and situations that confront children and adolescents with disabilities.

Acknowledgments

I am thankful for the assistance of many of my colleagues who provided reviews of this book in the manuscript phase. Bill Sharpton of the University of New Orleans assisted with a careful scrutiny of the cases and gave me innumerable suggestions for improving the content and format of this book. Others to whom I am grateful for their assistance include Barbara Baker and Susan Foster of Denver Public Schools, Carol Catardi of Jefferson County Public Schools, Mary Cronin of the University of New Orleans, and Catherine Curran of Metropolitan State College of Denver.

Very special thanks go to the other individuals who have taught me—year after year—the importance of working with families to achieve inclusion goals. In particular, I would like to thank Nancy Baesman, Jo Lynn Osborne, Donna Halcomb, Sharon Harris, Ellie Honeyman, Dottie Jennings, and Teresa Olmsted for helping me to better understand the importance of inclusion from a parent and family perspective.

I would also like to thank my mother, Patricia Carr, who is close to being a 30-year veteran of teaching special education and who holds more disability area credentials than anyone I know. Beginning, many years ago, as a teacher of students with visual impairments, she has continued to teach children and adolescents with numerous types of disabilities. In doing so, she has taught me the value of accepting individual differences while at the same time holding high expectations for achievement.

And finally, I owe gratitude to my husband, Stefan Kazmierski, who provides the support I need to do my work; and to my children, Alexandra and Nicholas Kazmierski, who are my inspiration and who so patiently waited for me to finish this manuscript.

Introduction

The Case Study Approach

The purpose of this book is to present a sampling of case studies that contain realistic problems for teacher education students to solve. This particular format was chosen because it provides the learner with the opportunity to *apply* information as opposed to merely memorizing it. Historically, case studies have played an important role in the training of many professions and have recently begun to attract increasing attention in the field of education as a means of bringing the role of theory closer to practice (Shulman, 1992). Several years ago, the significance of the case study approach was highlighted in the report *A Nation Prepared: Teachers for the 21st Century* (1989), which recommended that this teaching method be used as the major focus of instruction for teacher education programs. Goodlad (1990) seconded this recommendation when he also recommended the case study approach and suggested that teacher preparation could not be accomplished with "lecture-type courses and with the conventional reading list" (p. 293).

The case study format has the distinct advantage of providing the student with the opportunity to better understand the perspectives of others and to make educational decisions based upon a framework of this understanding (Merseth, 1992). As teacher education students, it is sometimes difficult to understand the feelings and attitudes of administrators, parents, and teachers of other specialty areas unless one assumes those particular roles and attempts to advocate for a position other than the one they might necessarily take as teachers. Another tremendous advantage of using the case study format is the resulting increase in student motivation that accompanies this instructional technique (Shulman, 1992).

Shulman (1992) described four different categories of cases, including case reports, case materials, case studies, and teaching cases. *Case reports* refer to firsthand accounts of experiences, whereas *case materials* refer to raw data used for interpretation of a particular problem. *Case Studies for Inclusive Schools* uses *case studies*, third-person descriptions of a situation, and *teaching cases*, accounts of a particular situation that present

a dilemma requiring a solution. These case studies could also be referred to as *case stories* (Ackerman, Maslin-Ostrowski, & Christensen, 1996). They are kept as brief as possible so that the learner has the opportunity to complete a greater number and can benefit from a wider variety of problem-solving situations. As Grossman (1992) suggested, consideration must be given to supplying enough detail to provide the context of the problem at hand, but the restraints of class time for discussion must also be kept in mind.

The Topic of Inclusion

The term *inclusion* means different things to different people, although most would agree that it generally refers to the idea of educating learners *with* disabilities in educational settings designed to serve the needs of learners *without* disabilities. Beyond that point, there is considerable disagreement as to exactly what inclusion *does* and *should* mean. As McCarthy (1994) aptly observed, there are few concepts that "are at the same time as attractive and threatening as 'inclusion'" (p. 1). Depending upon one's perspective, the inclusion movement has either promoted the dignity of individuals with disabilities through increased socialization experiences, or it is responsible for demoralizing general education teachers who are not provided the needed support to work with exceptional students and whose classrooms are fast becoming the new "dumping grounds" for special education. Segregation of individuals with disabilities is a recommendation that would find little, if any, support today; however, the determination of the extent of integration is another matter.

Hardman (1994) noted that "no single issue seems to polarize professionals and parents alike more than the debate regarding the extent to which students with disabilities should, or could be educated with their nondisabled peers in a regular education setting" (p. iii). Terms such as *full inclusion, partial inclusion, integration, regular education initiative,* and *mainstreaming* provide a great deal of confusion. Hardman further observed that this debate can be quite baffling for students in teacher education programs who are just starting to develop their ideas about the appropriateness of various settings for students with disabilities. Thus, it is the intention of this book to provide students with an overview of school problems related to inclusion from which they can acquire a better understanding of the multitude of issues that fall under this broad heading. It is *not* the purpose of *Case Studies for Inclusive Schools* to impress upon students that inclusion problems can be unilaterally resolved by promoting one particular viewpoint of inclusion. The case studies that were included in this book will hopefully lead students to the understanding that there can be no single recommendation for educational placement for all children and adolescents with disabilities. Each learner with a disability will have different needs—these needs must be addressed from the perspective of individuality rather than from the notion that there is one answer that is equally suited to all.

Organization of the Book

There were a number of different organizational formats that were initially considered when putting this book together. One of these formats involved organizing the cases together by age level, that is, early childhood, elementary, middle school, and high school. Another format involved the use of traditional special education categories as originally delineated in the Education for All Handicapped Children Act of 1975 (P.L. 94-142) and modified in the Individuals with Disabilities Education Act of 1990 (IDEA). Each of these formats has its strengths and limitations. It must be recognized that any classification of individuals by special education category is an artificial one that tends to engender stereotypical notions of a particular disability. A more realistic perception of disabilities could be illustrated by using a large, interconnected Venn diagram to display the prominence of the shared characteristics that are demonstrated across the traditional disability categories. However, in order to make this book "user friendly," the organizational format that ultimately was chosen focuses on the needs of the students with disabilities. This conceptualization is used by the Colorado State Department of Education for its special education teacher endorsement and service delivery (Swize, 1993). It is referred to as a needs-based model that focuses on the learner as opposed to special education categories. Although the chapters in this book do not parallel those of the Colorado model, the idea of organizing according to individual need is the same. The matrix on pages xvi–xviii, organized by level of intervention, is provided as a quick reference to major issues addressed in a particular case study.

Collaborative Problem-Solving Emphasis

Throughout the case studies included in this book, the intended focus is on the importance of individuals working together to generate solutions for problems in school settings. It is *not* the intention of this book to cast blame on certain individuals for holding viewpoints that are inconsistent with the goals of inclusion or to criticize those individuals for their viewpoints. On a prima facie level, certain attitudes may appear to be discriminatory, but often they are based more on ignorance than on any prejudicial feeling or any conscious desire to exclude individuals from the mainstream of the community. A careful examination of these attitudes within a problem-solving perspective often facilitates new understanding and acceptance of a different point of view.

Use of the Book

Case Studies for Inclusive Schools is intended to be used as a supplementary text for introductory courses in special education. It is also recommended for use with distance learning special education courses and could be used for school district inservices. This book was written to be used in two different ways: (a) in small-group activities during class time and (b) as individual activities to be completed before or after class for the purposes of discussion or evaluation of knowledge of course content. It should be noted that the case study activities cannot be satisfactorily completed without referring to other resources, such as the course text. Students must understand that the answers to these questions should be based on opinion that has a legitimate foundation. For example, it would not be sufficient for a student to recommend a certain solution for a child in question merely because of the student's feelings concerning the issue. The student would need to say that the recommendation is based on specific information in the book or other literature. Given that understanding, varying solutions should be encouraged and received in a manner that encourages diversity in problem solving.

The following explanation provides recommendations for case study uses.

Small-Group Activities

When this book is used for small-group activities during class, it is recommended that the first portion of the class be devoted to the case study content, for example, learning disabilities. The second portion of the class should then focus on the case study problem-solving activity to provide further understanding of difficulties encountered by children and adolescents with academic and language needs. It is also suggested that the small groups be formed according to the level of teacher preparation, that is, early childhood, elementary, or high school, in order to make the activity more relevant to the students. Most introductory special education classes are designed for all preparation levels. Use of this case study book allows students the opportunity to better understand issues that are related to developmental and educational level. The problems that accompany inclusion at the kindergarten level are vastly different from those confronted at the 10th-grade level.

There are two types of case study activities that can be accomplished in small-group settings. The first type of activity is *role playing*, in which the group members are asked to assume various roles and then reach a solution for the problem described in the case study. This kind of activity should produce a lively discussion that culminates in a resolution agreed upon by all participants. Students are then asked to summarize in writing the results of this problem-solving effort so they can refer to it later for study purposes. After the small-group activity, it is helpful for the entire class to listen to these summaries so they can be exposed to the different types of resolutions generated by the individual groups.

The second type of small-group activity is the *group case analysis*, which requires the students to answer questions about the problem presented in the case study. In order for this case analysis to be effective, the group must discuss each question and attempt to reach a consensus of opinion with regard to the issues at hand. It is not effective for the individuals to answer each question on their own and then discuss the answers when everyone has finished. The group as a whole must work through the questions in a collaborative manner, which is not unlike the process that occurs in the schools. If after doing this, an agreement cannot be reached, then the group should make a note of this fact and go on to the next question.

Individual Activities

There are two types of individual activities in this book. One type of individual activity focuses on answering the questions following each case study. This activity is designated as *individual* or *group case analysis*. The group method of problem solving was discussed earlier. Although there are definite advantages to group problem solving, one disadvantage concerns class time. There is usually not sufficient class time to cover the number of cases necessary to give students an appropriate overview of the complexity of problems that can occur in school settings. For this reason, it is recommended that students be assigned various case studies to complete outside of class. The individual case analysis is also recommended when this book is used as a resource for a distance learning course. The completed work can then be discussed in class, or it can be turned in to be evaluated by the instructor. When it is turned in for evaluation purposes, it is recommended that the instructor use a pass/fail system of grading. Although there are some knowledge-level questions included in these case analyses, for most of the questions that are raised, there are no right or wrong answers. Students can demonstrate their ability to apply course content by adequately supporting their opinions with facts, such as legal precedents and recommendations from literature focusing on that particular topic. When these arguments are presented in a logical and thoughtful manner and in clear narrative writing, they should receive a passing grade.

The other individual activity included in this case study book involves the use of a narrative writing assignment in which the student is asked to provide a detailed analysis of a case. These activities are helpful because they allow the student to demonstrate an ability to identify and prioritize specific problems, and then to devise workable solutions. This activity can be used as a work sample for the course or as an artifact for a teacher education portfolio.

Matrix of Case Studies

Early Childhood and Primary Level

	Age	Assess-ment	Instruc-tional	Legal	Family	Transi-tion	Place-ment	Cul-tural	IEP
Antonio	7		X		X		X		
Susanne	5	X	X		X		X		
Eli	7		X	X	X		X		
Lemar	6		X		X		X	X	
Sammy	8		X		X			X	
Casey	8	X	X		X				
Jenny	7		X	X	X				
Joseph	6		X						
Levonda	6		X		X		X		X
Rinna	5		X		X		X		X
Denisa	7		X	X	X		X	X	
Michael	8		X	X	X		X		
Nicole	5		X	X	X		X		
Travis	4		X	X	X		X		
Hannah	5	X	X		X				
Kayla	4		X		X		X		
Seth	6		X	X	X		X		
Amber	7	X	X		X		X		
Brenna	6		X	X	X		X		
Ted	6		X		X		X		
Lily	5		X	X	X		X		

(continues)

Elementary

	Age	Assess-ment	Instruc-tional	Legal	Family	Transi-tion	Place-ment	Cul-tural	IEP
Jessie	8		X		X		X		
Juan	10	X	X		X			X	X
Kevin	11	X	X		X		X		
Madeline	9	X	X		X		X		X
Elizabeth	10		X		X				
Hwa-Fang	9	X	X	X	X	X	X	X	
Keisha	9		X	X	X		X		
Jason	10		X		X		X		
Maria	9	X	X		X				
Ramon	9		X		X				
Jody	9		X		X			X	
Miguel	10		X				X	X	
Mitchell	11		X	X	X		X		
Jamal	10		X		X		X		
Janell	10		X		X		X		
Leroy	9		X		X				
Richard	9		X				X	X	
Veru	10		X		X		X		X
Emilio	9	X	X		X		X	X	X
Valerie	10		X	X	X		X		
Arletha	10	X	X				X	X	
Jeffrey	8		X		X		X		
Marcus	11	X	X		X		X	X	

(continues)

Middle/High School

	Age	Assess-ment	Instruc-tional	Legal	Family	Transi-tion	Place-ment	Cul-tural	IEP
Aaron	17		X		X	X			
Marta	18	X	X	X	X	X	X		
Mission Heights	–	X	X						
Geraldo	13	X	X						
Peter	15		X	X	X	X	X		
Vincent	18	X	X		X	X	X		
David	13		X		X		X		
LeShawn	15		X	X				X	
Joel	17		X		X		X		
Lionel	14		X	X	X		X	X	
Serena	16		X		X		X		
Chad	12		X		X				X
Melissa	13		X	X	X				
Robert	16		X	X	X	X	X		
Tom	14		X		X				
Mark	12		X		X		X		
Yuri	16	X	X		X		X	X	
Greg	13	X	X	X	X		X		
Paul	16	X	X		X	X	X		
Jake	14		X		X	X	X	X	
Karen	17		X		X		X		
Lauren	13	X	X	X	X			X	X
Markell	12		X				X	X	
Jenna	13		X		X	X	X		
Leo	15		X		X	X	X		
Margo	14		X	X	X				

References

Ackerman, R., Maslin-Ostrowski, P., & Christensen, C. (1996). Case stories: Telling tales about schools. *Educational Leadership, 53*(6), 21–23.

Carnegie Task Force on Teaching as a Profession. (1989). *A nation prepared: Teachers for the 21st century.* New York: Carnegie Forum on Education and the Economy, Carnegie Corporation.

Education for All Handicapped Children Act of 1975, 20 U.S.C. § 1400 *et seq.*

Goodlad, J. I. (1990). *Teachers for our nation's schools.* San Francisco: Jossey-Bass.

Grossman, P. L. (1992). Teaching and learning with cases: Unanswered questions. In J. H. Shulman (Ed.), *Case methods in teacher education* (pp. 227–239). New York: Teachers College Press.

Hardman, M. L. (1994). *Inclusion: Issues of educating students with disabilities in regular education settings.* Boston: Allyn & Bacon.

Individuals with Disabilities Education Act of 1990, 20 U.S.C. § 1400 *et seq.*

McCarthy, M. (1994). Inclusion and the law: Recent judicial developments. *Research Bulletin, 13,* 1.

Mercer, J. R., & Lewis, J. F. (1978). *System of multicultural pluralistic assessment.* San Antonio, TX: The Psychological Corp.

Merseth, K. (1992). Cases for decision making in teacher education. In J. H. Shulman (Ed.), *Case methods in teacher education* (pp. 50–63). New York: Teachers College Press.

Raven, J. C., Court, J. H., & Raven, J. (1986). *Raven's Progressive Matrices.* London: Lewis.

Shulman, L. S. (1992). Toward a pedagogy of cases. In J. H. Shulman (Ed.), *Case methods in teacher education* (pp. 1–30). New York: Teachers College Press.

Sparrow, S. S., Balla, D. A., & Cicchetti, D. V. (1984). *Vineland Adaptive Behavior Scales.* Circle Pines, MN: American Guidance.

Stanford Achievement Test (8th ed.). (1990). San Antonio, TX: The Psychological Corp.

Swize, M. (1993). Colorado's Needs Based Model. In Colorado Department of Special Education (Ed.), *Instructionally differentiated programming: A needs based approach for students with behavior disorders* (pp. 6–13). Denver: Colorado Department of Education.

Thorndike, R. L., Hagen, E. P., & Sattler, J. M. (1986). *Stanford-Binet Intelligence Scale* (4th ed.). Chicago: Riverside.

Wechsler, D. (1967). *Wechsler Preschool and Primary Scale of Intelligence.* San Antonio, TX: The Psychological Corp.

Wechsler, D. (1974). *Wechsler Intelligence Scale for Children–Revised.* San Antonio, TX: The Psychological Corp.

Wechsler, D. (1991). *Wechsler Intelligence Scale for Children–Third Edition.* San Antonio, TX: The Psychological Corp.

Academic and Language Needs

CHAPTER 1

Aaron

Aaron is a 17-year-old senior at Chatsworth Senior High School where he is currently enrolled in the life skills program. This is a transition program designed to meet the career and community living goals of students with disabilities. These students spend their mornings at the school learning functional skills and their afternoons working on a job in the community. Aaron has spent the last 3 months working at a family business where he was eventually to be employed on a full-time basis when he finished school at Chatsworth. This is a machine parts business that Aaron's father and his partner have owned for 20 years.

Yesterday Aaron's father, Mr. Martinson, came in to see Mr. Larriva, who is Aaron's life skills teacher, and Mr. Fahey, who is Aaron's vocational counselor. He was extremely upset, almost to the point of being tearful. After 3 months of having Aaron work part-time at his machine parts store, he has discovered that his son does not have the skills necessary to keep this entry-level position in the business. His partner of 20 years has asked him to fire Aaron, and Mr. Martinson knows his partner is right. Included in the long list of Aaron's job problems were complaints about his inability to follow directions, inability to organize, and lack of motivation. One example of organizational problems had to do with the warehouse. When Aaron was asked to clean up the warehouse, he would go inside, pick up any loose parts, and then put them in whatever box happened to be closest. Consequently, different machine parts were being mixed together, causing major problems with orders. When his attention was called to this problem, Aaron did not seem to see that the parts looked different and therefore should not be in the same box.

Mr. Martinson talked at length about other problems with organization and misuse of time. For example, on one occasion Aaron was asked to take all the orange-colored files out of the file cabinets and place them in a separate box. Instead of pulling out only the orange files, Aaron took all the files out of each drawer and spread them around on the office floor. Mr. Martinson was astonished when he walked into the office and saw the mess. Aaron was perplexed by his father's reaction because he felt he was doing a more thorough job this way. However, when Aaron tried to put the current files back into the cabinet in alphabetical order, he found that he could not. He became so frustrated that he dropped the task and went on to something else back in the warehouse. Mr. Martinson had his secretary clean up the filing mess because he didn't want his partner to see it. According to Mr. Martinson, the worst part of the whole situation is that Aaron doesn't even seem to recognize when he does something wrong, nor does he show any desire to improve or to learn from his mistakes. Since Aaron has come to work, Mr. Martinson has felt that he does nothing all day except put out fires.

This whole experience has caused significant despair for Mr. Martinson. As he told Mr. Larriva and Mr. Fahey, "If my son doesn't have the skills to work for me in this type of job, what can he do?" He further told the teachers that he doesn't even understand what a learning disability is or whether it can be cured. It was his understanding that Aaron would always have problems in school, but no one ever told him that he wouldn't be able to hold down a job. Mr. Martinson asked the teachers if there was anything he could do to help his son.

Background Information:

Aaron was diagnosed as having a learning disability in the third grade. The special education evaluation report indicated that Aaron had a receptive language weakness, which was manifested in difficulty following directions. A reading disability, a lack of visual–motor coordination, and attentional deficits were also identified. Aaron was placed in a self-contained learning disabilities classroom from the fourth grade to the sixth grade. During middle school he attended a resource program where he received help for 50 minutes each day. For the first 3 years of high school, he was placed into low-ability classes where he received supplementary help from special education teachers on a tutorial basis. Aaron was considered to be an ideal candidate for the life skills program.

Aaron's special education teachers always felt that he was a hard worker; however, that evaluation was not shared by some of his regular education teachers who described him as "lazy, inattentive, disorganized, and unmotivated," among other things. His parents pro-

vided him with a good deal of support. Records indicated that both Mr. and Mrs. Martinson were present at the initial staffing and at every annual review conference for the past 8 years.

Aaron has enjoyed the life skills program at Chatsworth, and he has expressed a great deal of satisfaction in "working for my dad." Both Mr. Fahey and Mr. Larriva are surprised that things are not going well at the machine parts business. On the occasions that Mr. Fahey visited the site, he had the impression that Aaron was working hard. Aaron has mentioned on several occasions that he wants to hurry and graduate from the life skills program so that he can help out full time at the parts business. Aaron has the impression that his services are greatly needed at his father's business.

 ## Case Study Activities

PART I:
ROLE PLAYING

Break into groups of four or five. Simulate a conference at which Aaron, his teachers, and his father discuss how to resolve this problem. The following roles should be assumed by group members: Aaron, Mr. Martinson, Mr. Larriva, Mr. Fahey, and Mrs. Martinson (an optional role). Provide a written summary of the resolution for Aaron's problem.

Resolution

_____

_____

_____

_____

_____

_____

PART II:
INDIVIDUAL OR GROUP CASE ANALYSIS

Answer the following questions and be prepared to discuss them in class.

1. How is it possible that Mr. Martinson has attended all of those school meetings over the course of 9 years and yet does not understand his son's learning disability? How might this misunderstanding have been avoided?

_____

_____

_____

_____

_____

_____

_____

_____

_____

2. Do you believe that Aaron has motivation problems? Why or why not?

_____

_____

_____

_____

_____

_____

_____

3. Why do you think that Aaron's special education teachers saw Aaron in a different light than his regular education teachers?

_____

_____

_____

_____

_____

_____

_____

4. Which of the problems identified in Aaron's original special education evaluation may be interfering with his job performance at the machine parts business?

_____

_____

_____

_____

_____

_____

_____

_____

_____

5. How do you account for the idea that Aaron believes he is doing an excellent job at the parts business when, in reality, his father is getting ready to fire him?

_____

_____

_____

_____

_____

_____

_____

_____

_____

_____

_____

6. What could Mr. Larriva and Mr. Fahey do to assist Aaron in this situation? What can they do to help this family?

_____

_____

_____

_____

_____

_____

_____

_____

_____

Antonio

Antonio is a 7-year-old first-grade student at Costilla Elementary School. Last year, in kindergarten, he was diagnosed with Tourette's syndrome. Antonio exhibits complex vocal and motor tics. In terms of his vocal tic behaviors, Antonio makes animal sounds, spits, belches, and hums. Other tic behaviors include sticking out his tongue, sucking his thumb, poking, and pinching. Antonio also demonstrates coprolalia (the uncontrolled use of obscene language). He has poor language skills, with his expressive language being placed at the 4-year-old level and his receptive language at the 5-year-old level. Antonio has limited readiness skills. He does not consistently identify letters or numbers, and he has a very difficult time with visual–motor skills, such as cutting and writing. He also has poor attention skills and some degree of impulsivity. There is no mention of possible strengths in either his evaluation report or his cumulative file.

Background Information:

Antonio had a very difficult time in kindergarten. His vocal and motor tics interfered with classroom expectations to the extent that the school nurse was assigned full care of Antonio for the 2½ hours of kindergarten. (The school did not have funds available to hire an aide for this class.) He was referred for evaluation during the first week of school. This evaluation concluded that Antonio had Tourette's syndrome as well as learning disabilities. Because the psychologist and the kindergarten teacher, Mrs. Vigil, viewed the behavior associated with Tourette's as the primary disability, it was recommended that Antonio be placed in a special school that serves children with severe emotional disturbances. Mrs. Vigil held the opinion that Antonio could refrain from the tic behaviors if he chose to do so. She frequently punished him for these tics. For example, any vocal tics that she considered to be disruptive to the class were identified as good cause for an extended time-out in the office. The parents declined special school placement because they live right across the street from Costilla Elementary, and they want Antonio to go to the same school as his three siblings. Although they were very unhappy with Mrs. Vigil's treatment of Antonio, they felt and continue to feel that he belongs in his neighborhood school. They are hopeful that Antonio will have a better experience in Mrs. Selby's first-grade class.

 Case Study Activity

INDIVIDUAL OR GROUP CASE ANALYSIS

Answer the following questions and be prepared to discuss them in class.

1. What resources can Mrs. Selby use to prepare to meet Antonio's needs? Name at least two different resources and tell why these might be effective.

_____

_____

_____

_____

_____

_____

_____

_____

2. What can Mrs. Selby do about Antonio's tic behaviors? Give four specific suggestions.

_____

_____

_____

_____

_____

_____

_____

3. Why do you think that there was no mention of Antonio's strengths in his evaluation records? How could Mrs. Selby identify this child's strengths and use them to plan his educational program?

_____

_____

_____

_____

_____

_____

_____

4. Do you think that a regular education setting is more appropriate than the special school for students with emotional disturbance that was recommended following Antonio's evaluation? Why or why not?

_____

_____

_____

_____

_____

_____

_____

5. Do you think that Antonio's kindergarten program was appropriate? Why or why not?

_____

_____

_____

_____

_____

_____

_____

6. If you were Mrs. Selby, what specific stategies would you use to increase Antonio's visual–motor skills? Give four specific strategies.

_____

_____

_____

_____

_____

_____

7. What is Tourette's syndrome? Is it typical for a child with Tourette's to also have learning disabilities and attentional problems?

_____

_____

_____

_____

_____

_____

_____

Jessie

Jessie is an 8-year-old third grader at Eastlake Elementary. He was diagnosed with a learning disability at the age of 7. Jessie is in Mr. Stewart's third-grade class for a full instructional day, and he receives the help of a special education teacher, Mrs. Panno, for 50 minutes per day. Mr. Stewart and Mrs. Panno are currently in the process of planning Jessie's language arts program.

Background Information:

Jessie's first-grade teacher referred him for special education evaluation. She was concerned because he could not identify letters or basic geometric shapes. Additionally, he seemed to have difficulty learning sounds in the beginning phonics program. The pupil assessment team determined that Jessie did indeed have normal potential (IQ of 115), but he had significant deficits in both visual and auditory perception. In spite of these deficits, Jessie's vocabulary and comprehension of connected language were well above expectancy for a child of his age. The assessment team also identified a learning disability at this time, but Jessie's parents, Mr. and Mrs. Wagner, refused special education placement. They felt that since Jessie was such a bright child with good verbal skills, they did not want to label him with a problem that might eventually take care of itself. They believed that given additional time to develop, Jessie would catch up with his first-grade peers.

By the middle of Jessie's second-grade year, he had still made little progress. Although he could identify many letters, he could not consistently recognize any of the vocabulary that his peers read, nor could he put any sounds together with letters to consistently create appropriate phoneme–grapheme correspondences. Mr. and Mrs. Wagner reconsidered his educational curriculum and asked that he receive special education services starting in the third grade.

 ## Case Study Activity

INDIVIDUAL OR GROUP CASE ANALYSIS

Answer the following questions and be prepared to discuss them in class.

1. What type of reading program would you recommend for Jessie? Why do you think this type of program would work best for him?

_____

_____

_____

_____

_____

_____

_____

2. Now that Jessie is receiving special education services, do you think he will be able to make normal progress in reading?

_____

_____

_____

_____

_____

_____

3. Would it be a good idea for Jessie to be pulled out of his third-grade class to receive intensive reading instruction, or should Mrs. Panno work with him in Mr. Stewart's class on the curriculum that the other third graders are working on? Give three reasons for your answer.

_____

_____

_____

_____

_____

_____

4. Should Jessie have started special education services in first grade? Can you explain why Mr. and Mrs. Wagner felt it would be better for Jessie not to be identified as a special needs child? Is it possible that learning problems can be alleviated with additional maturity?

_____

_____

_____

_____

_____

_____

5. Write a lesson plan for Mr. Stewart's third-grade class with the objective of teaching the students to identify and comprehend 10 new vocabulary words from a science lesson. Add an adaptation to the plan indicating how this basic lesson could be modified to achieve the objective in Jessie's case.

_____

_____

_____

_____

_____

_____

Juan

Juan is a 10-year-old third grader at Villano Elementary School. He is a bilingual child who was recently placed in special education. Juan is considered to be Spanish dominant for receptive language but English dominant for expressive language. He was tested in both Spanish and English for the special education evaluation. His *Wechsler Intelligence Scale for Children–Third Edition* (WISC–III; Wechsler, 1991) profile indicated that his verbal IQ was 82, while his performance IQ was 74. Academic testing revealed a reading disability. Juan is currently reading on a second-grade level in English, and his Spanish reading is at approximately the same level. Although Juan demonstrated knowledge of word attack skills, his sight word vocabulary was considerably lower because of numerous reversals in his reading. His math skills appear to be somewhat higher, at approximately the early third-grade level. Other areas of weakness that were noted in the testing were illegible handwriting and poor eye–hand coordination.

At the staffing, Juan's teachers from last year commented on some of his problems in the classroom. Juan's reading teacher, Ms. Renfro, felt that many of his reading problems were due to visual confusion; he frequently reversed both letters and words. His second–grade teacher from last year, Mrs. Fernandez, noted that he had a very difficult time with any board work. She said that he could not copy accurately from the board. She also noted that his handwriting was so poor that it was difficult to evaluate his written work. Mrs. Fernandez also expressed concern regarding Juan's socialization. She identified him as a loner who did not seem to have any friends. She was concerned because he was so reticent in class. It was difficult to get him to speak up in oral discussions.

Background Information:

Juan and his mother, Mrs. Gallegos, came to the United States when Juan was 2 years old. Mr. Gallegos was to join the family later, but he was killed in a tragic car accident on his way to meet them. Although this accident occurred more than 8 years ago, family members say that Mrs. Gallegos has never recovered and has suffered from severe depression since that time. Juan and his mother live alone. An elderly aunt who lives down the street visits them often and helps to care for the family. Although they have many other relatives in the city, they rarely visit them because of Mrs. Gallegos' illness. She is bedridden much of the time, and she needs Juan to care for her. Juan is not allowed to go out of the yard because Mrs. Gallegos fears for his safety.

Juan started kindergarten a year late. His mother told the school she did not understand that he was to begin at the age of 5. Although his kindergarten teacher wanted to have him repeat kindergarten because his socialization, language, and visual–motor skills were so poor, she decided against this recommendation because he was already a year older than most of the other children. A year later, his first-grade teacher felt that she could not let him go on to second-grade because he was doing so poorly. His second-grade teacher referred him for the special education evaluation because his work in her classroom was well below that of his peers. She decided not to recommend retention because he had been identified as having a learning disability.

 Case Study Activities

PART I:
ROLE PLAYING

Break into groups of four or five. Simulate an Individualized Educational Program (IEP) meeting in which Juan's educational needs are addressed. Use the IEP form included on page 13 to write these goals. The following roles should be assumed by group members: Mrs. Gallegos, Mrs. Valdez (Juan's aunt), Mrs. Patrice (Juan's third-grade teacher), Ms. Grebar (Juan's special education teacher), and Mrs. Renfro (Juan's second-grade reading teacher—an optional role). During this meeting the group should be sure to: (a) review current functioning, (b) identify strengths and weaknesses, (c) develop short and long term goals, (d) describe possible teaching strategies that will be used to achieve these goals, (e) explain the services to be provided, and (f) determine responsibility with regard to carrying out the educational plan.

PART II:
INDIVIDUAL OR GROUP CASE ANALYSIS

Answer the following questions and be prepared to discuss them in class.

1. Explain what is meant by the description, "Juan is considered to be Spanish dominant for receptive language and English dominant for expressive language." How could this influence Juan's classroom performance?

_____

_____

_____

_____

_____

_____

_____

2. What kinds of language arts activities can Juan's third-grade teacher use to assist his achievement in this area? Give four different strategies.

_____

_____

_____

_____

_____

_____

_____

3. What kinds of strategies can Juan's third-grade teacher use to encourage his socialization? Give four different examples.

_____

_____

_____

_____

_____

_____

_____

4. What can the school do to help this family? Are there any community resources that might provide assistance to Juan and his mother?

_____

_____

_____

_____

_____

_____

5. When completing an assessment on a bilingual child, such as Juan, how does the assessment team decide whether the educational problems are the result of the language difference or a learning disability?

_____

_____

_____

_____

_____

_____

_____

Kevin

Kevin is an 11-year-old fifth grader at Riverbend Elementary School. He has been receiving resource room special education services for a learning disability in the area of reading for the past 3 years. This year the pupil assessment team has recommended that Kevin be provided special education services in the regular classroom. They have suggested that the special education teacher, Mr. Wernicke, work in collaboration with the regular classroom teacher, Mrs. Verlo, to meet Kevin's educational needs. The team feels that Kevin should not be taken out of his regular classroom because he misses too much of the instruction that takes place in that setting.

Mrs. Verlo thinks that this change in placement is a good idea, and she is looking forward to having some extra assistance during language arts. She has just finished reading an article about the value of regular and special education co-teaching in an elementary education journal, and she is eager to try this type of cooperative approach. She also believes that she will learn a good deal about special education methodology by working closely with Mr. Wernicke. Mr. Wernicke is less enthusiastic about this idea. He believes that the greatest gains in reading are made as a result of intensive remedial instruction in a one-to-one situation. He doesn't really think that any good can come from the type of team teaching recommended by the assessment team.

School District #1
Individualized Educational Program

Student: _____

Current Functioning	Long-Term Goals	Short-Term Objectives

Background Information:

Mr. Wernicke has been Kevin's teacher for the last 3 years. He has been using a remedial phonics approach to reading instruction. He is a very conscientious teacher who works diligently to achieve IEP goals. However, in spite of all Mr. Wernicke's efforts, Kevin has made little progress in the area of phonics. Kevin was reading a year below grade level when he was identified as having a reading disability 3 years ago. His latest composite reading scores, which were compiled for annual review, indicated that he was reading approximately 1½ years below expectancy. While his scores for reading comprehension appear to be showing improvement, his basic reading skills (sight word vocabulary, syllabication, and phonics) are much lower.

Kevin's mother, Mrs. Mickelson, is very upset because he still isn't reading on grade level. Although she likes Mr. Wernicke and feels that he is a dedicated teacher, she is frustrated that Kevin doesn't seem to be making the progress that she anticipated when she signed the placement papers for his special education services 3 years ago. Mrs. Mickelson is distressed that the gap between grade level and reading level is actually widening instead of narrowing. She supports the pupil assessment team's recommendation to keep Kevin in Mrs. Verlo's classroom for language arts, even though Mr. Wernicke has encouraged her to object to this plan.

 Case Study Activity

INDIVIDUAL OR GROUP CASE ANALYSIS

Answer the following questions and be prepared to discuss them in class.

1. Why has the gap between Kevin's reading level and grade level actually widened in spite of the intensive remedial reading program provided to this student? Should Mr. Wernicke be held responsible for Kevin's lack of progress?

_____

_____

_____

_____

_____

_____

2. Why do you think that Mr. Wernicke is so resistant to Kevin's full-time placement in the regular classroom? Give three reasons.

_____

_____

_____

_____

_____

_____

_____

3. How could a collaborative teaching program benefit Kevin as well as the other fifth graders in Mrs. Verlo's classroom? Give four examples.

_____

_____

_____

_____

_____

_____

4. What you do think about Mr. Wernicke's method of reading instruction? Do you think Kevin will ever be able to use phonics with any degree of proficiency? Why or why not?

_____

_____

_____

_____

_____

_____

5. Do you think that Mr. Wernicke and Mrs. Verlo will be able to work together in this situation? What obstacles may interfere? If you were the principal of this school, how would you assist these teachers in this endeavor?

_____

_____

_____

_____

_____

_____

6. Explain how Mr. Wernicke and Mrs. Verlo could develop a language arts unit focusing on Black History Month. How could they share responsibilities for this unit? Develop a sample lesson plan to explain how these teachers could work together for the benefit of Kevin as well as the other fifth graders. In this plan, be sure to specify which teacher will be responsible for each activity and what modifications will be necessary.

_____

_____

_____

_____

_____

_____

_____

Madeline

Madeline is a 9-year-old fourth grader at Venetian Hills Elementary School. She was diagnosed as having a learning disability in first grade and was placed in a self-contained special education classroom for second and third grades. Reading problems and social problems have been identified as major concerns for this student. This year the school district has decided to rearrange its service delivery model for special education. They will no longer be offering self-contained classrooms for students with learning disabilities. Self-contained classrooms will be reserved only for students with severe disabilities.

Madeline's special education teacher, Mrs. Jenkins, feels that Madeline has done well for the past 2 years. She is somewhat concerned that the transition from special education to regular education will be very challenging for this student. If Mrs. Jenkins had been given a choice, she would not have mainstreamed Madeline for another couple of years. She is especially concerned about her social skills, which are well below that which one would expect of a fourth grader. Madeline has made friends with a student with Down syndrome and a first grader with autistic-like tendencies. She seems very comfortable with this social group, and Mrs. Jenkins doesn't know how she will fare with her fourth-grade peers. When Madeline is involved in activities with her nondisabled peers, she complains that they pick on her. She has been given the nickname of "robot girl" because of the way she speaks, which is in a flat tone that is lacking in the usual inflections. This is a distinctive characteristic that is obvious to everyone who comes into contact with Madeline. She also has unusual social language, which causes her to stand out from her peers. Whenever she speaks to Mrs. Jenkins, she begins by saying, "Pardon me, if you will." Mrs. Jenkins is well aware that Madeline uses this phrase over and over again throughout the day, but she has not been able to change this behavior. Almost all of Madeline's language comes out as if it were rotely memorized instead of being formulated for the purpose at hand. When Mrs. Jenkins has gently talked to her about using more inflection, Madeline becomes very anxious and says things like, "Pardon me, but this is how I talk," and "I don't know why everyone wants to change me . . . Pardon me, if you will, but this is the way I want to talk."

Madeline's parents, Mr. and Mrs. Tyler, are very glad that she will be getting out of the special education classroom. They were never comfortable with the fact that their daughter's classmates all had disabilities. They would like her to experience a more typical classroom environment where she might have the opportunity to model what they refer to as "normal" behaviors. They know that their daughter has some unusual behaviors, but they are still hoping that she will grow out of these if given the appropriate environment. Mr. and Mrs. Tyler are a bit dissatisfied with the school district's approach to Madeline's education. They know their daughter is different, but they don't understand why everybody wants to focus on her differences.

Madeline's fourth-grade teacher, Mr. Cervantes, is hesitant about having Madeline in the classroom full time. She strikes him as a very unusual child. Her physical features are similar to that of a child with Down syndrome, but he has been told that she does not have this disorder. He is really bothered by her flat, strange language. Mr. Cervantes describes Madeline to his colleagues as a "child who's really out of it." Madeline has only been in the classroom for a couple of weeks now, and the other fourth graders have made it clear that they don't want anything to do with her. He doesn't blame them. Mr. Cervantes doesn't know how to work with a child like this, and he's going to make this clear at the upcoming IEP meeting. Mr. Cervantes is going to suggest that Mrs. Jenkins pull Madeline out for resource help for most of the instructional day, and he hopes that she will be in art, music, or physical education classes for the rest of the day so that he won't have to worry about this "problem." He knows he can count on Mr. Egars, the principal, for support because Mr. Egars doesn't think much of inclusion either. Mr. Egars told the faculty that he wanted to house all the special education children in the mobile units behind the building this year. He seemed upset when the superintendent decided to do away with self-contained special education classrooms.

Background Information:

Madeline's birth was premature by 6 weeks. She was a tiny baby, weighing about 3½ pounds. Her pediatrician ordered genetic testing because there was some initial concern that she had Down syndrome. The tests came back negative, much to the relief of the parents.

Madeline experienced difficulty during the first year of life. She was identified as "failure to thrive" and was hospitalized for this condition three times before she turned 1 year of age. She did better developmentally during her preschool years, but she still lagged behind her peers. Mrs. Tyler always thought that something was wrong with Madeline's development, but her pediatrician assured her that she was doing fine. Madeline's kindergarten teacher referred her for special education evaluation after the first week of school. She was certain that there was something very wrong with Madeline's development based on the way she looked and acted.

The special education evaluation team identified major strengths in auditory processing for sounds (Madeline's word attack skills were at the third-grade level) and visual–motor performance. Weaknesses were identified in language comprehension. It was determined that she should receive speech and language services during that kindergarten year. At the end of the year, Madeline's performance in reading and math was so low, it was determined that a self-contained special education classroom might be the best placement for this child.

Recent testing revealed that Madeline's composite reading score places her at the second-grade level (reading comprehension 1.2, sight word vocabulary 2.3, and word attack 4.1). Math scores indicated that computations were at the 3.4 grade level, but math reasoning lagged behind at the 1.3 grade level. Receptive language was 2 years below expectancy with noted weaknesses in understanding connected language and strengths in the area of single word vocabulary. The assessment team also noted that Madeline's social skills were very atypical, and training in this area should be perceived as a priority.

 ## Case Study Activities

PART I:
ROLE PLAYING

Break into groups of five and simulate an IEP meeting in which Madeline's educational needs are addressed. Use the IEP form included on page 20 to write these goals. The following roles should be assumed by group members: Mr. Tyler, Mrs. Tyler, Mrs. Jenkins, Mr. Cervantes, and Mr. Egars. During this meeting, the group should be sure to: (a) review current functioning, (b) identify strengths and weaknesses, (c) develop short and long term goals, (d) describe possible teaching strategies that will be used to achieve these goals, (e) explain the services to be provided, and (f) determine responsibility with regard to carrying out the educational plan.

PART II:
INDIVIDUAL OR GROUP CASE ANALYSIS

Answer the following questions and be prepared to discuss them in class.

1. Why do you think Mr. Egars wanted the special education students to be separated from the main school building? What would be the advantages and disadvantages of such an arrangement?

_____

_____

_____

_____

_____

_____

_____

2. Do you think that Mr. and Mrs. Tyler are unrealistic about their daughter's differences? Do you think that school systems typically emphasize the differences between students with disabilities and their nondisabled peers? Why or why not?

_____

_____

_____

_____

_____

_____

_____

3. Why do you think Madeline prefers the company of children who have disabilities? As Madeline's teacher, how would you encourage socialization with her fourth-grade peers? Describe four different strategies you would use, and explain why you think these would be effective.

_____

_____

_____

_____

_____

_____

_____

4. As Madeline's teacher, how would you assist her in language development? Describe four strategies you would use in this case, and explain why you think these would be effective.

_____

_____

_____

_____

_____

_____

_____

_____

_____

_____

_____

_____

5. Do you think it would be more beneficial for Madeline to be pulled out and placed in a resource situation for most of her academic instruction or to stay in Mr. Cervantes' classroom and have Mrs. Jenkins come in and assist her? Explain your response.

_____

_____

_____

_____

_____

_____

_____

_____

_____

School District #1
Individualized Educational Program

Student: _____

Current Functioning	Long-Term Goals	Short-Term Objectives

Marta

Marta is an 18-year-old senior at Essex High School. She was diagnosed as learning disabled at the age of 7. During her school career, she was originally staffed into a self-contained classroom and then later transferred to a resource program. Marta's specific learning disability was identified in the area of reading. After 12 years of special education services, she is reading at the fourth-grade level.

Marta recently received her letter indicating that she will graduate with her class. This letter served as a "wake-up call" for her parents, Mr. and Mrs. Martinez, who promptly hired an independent evaluator to test Marta. The evaluation indicated that she was achieving at the fourth-grade level in reading and at the sixth-grade level in math. Mr. and Mrs. Martinez are furious because they feel that in spite of Marta's potential (IQ of 135), she is not prepared to do anything after graduation. They went to the principal, Mr. Vigil, with their concerns and suggested that Marta's IEP goals have not been met. Mr. Vigil dismissed their concerns by saying that Marta did not meet her goals because she was an unmotivated student. This comment made the Martinez family even angrier. They went home and started investigating private schools. They have recently written a letter to the superintendent, Mr. Greer, describing their problem with the school and demanding that the district pick up the $25,000 bill for a year at a residential school that specializes in treating students who are severely learning disabled. Mr. Greer has responded by telling Mr. Vigil to set up a meeting to resolve this problem immediately.

Background Information:

During Marta's third-grade year, the district implemented a strict, competency-based achievement program. They put a great deal of effort into publicizing this program. They gave district-wide parent information sessions explaining the details of this program, which was named Accountability Plus. Parents were told that these new criteria would ensure high standards for all students in the district. The district did not publicly say anything about excluding special education students from Accountability Plus, but, in reality, it was the district's policy not to have these students participate in the examinations for this standards program. The rationale apparently focused on the idea that special education students were incapable of meeting these standards, so they should be socially promoted. Their logic was that the district could not keep students who were mentally retarded in the second or third grade for most of their school experience.

 ## Case Study Activities

PART I:
ROLE PLAYING

Break into groups of four or five. Simulate a conference in which this problem is resolved. Assume one of the following roles: Mr. Greer, Mr. Vigil, Mr. Martinez, Marta, and Mrs. Martinez (an optional role). Provide a written summary of the resolution.

Mr. Greer, superintendent

Viewpoint: I don't understand these parents. Did they really want their daughter to fail every grade? Good grief, if we held this student to district standards, she would still be in the fourth grade. There's no way that we're going to pay $25,000 for this girl to go to that fancy private school. The school board will have my head if that happens!

Mr. Vigil, principal

Viewpoint: How did I end up with this mess? It's not my fault that this kid was socially promoted all the way through the elementary and middle school grades. What am I supposed to do, send her back to the fourth grade? Why isn't the special education director here? She should take responsibility for this mess. What are they doing in special education if they're not addressing standards? Why am I taking the heat for this debacle? I hope I don't lose my job over this. I don't want to end up back in the classroom.

Marta, student

Viewpoint: What am I doing here? I told my parents I didn't want to come. I can't believe that my parents are making such a big deal about this. So what if I can't read? I'm smarter than most of the kids in this school. I can get by just fine. My parents are nuts if they think I'm going to some weird school for another year after I've already graduated. Give me a break!

Mr. Martinez, Marta's father

Viewpoint: I'm not going to stand for this. This is outrageous! I've been paying property taxes for 25 years to support this school system and their fiascoes. Accountability Plus is a sham. These people are going to pay for this mess. What kind of a life is my child going to have with a fourth-grade reading level?

Mrs. Martinez, Marta's mother

Viewpoint: Marta's going to end up like me—with no choices except an early marriage. I failed all the way through school and ended up being graduated because I brown-nosed my way through enough classes to pass the requirements. It's my fault that Marta can't read—she has the very same problem that I have. She deserves better, and I'm going to get it for her. My parents couldn't do anything for me, but I'm determined to do something for her.

Resolution

_____

_____

_____

_____

_____

_____

_____

_____

PART II:
INDIVIDUAL OR GROUP CASE ANALYSIS

Answer the following questions and be prepared to discuss them in class.

1. Do you think that a student who does not meet school district requirements should receive a diploma or a certificate of attendance? Explain your response.

_____

_____

_____

_____

_____

_____

_____

_____

2. Do you think that social promotion for students with disabilities is a good idea? Why or why not?

_____

_____

_____

_____

_____

_____

_____

3. How is it possible that Marta has a superior IQ and yet has failed to learn to read beyond an elementary school achievement level? If she had been provided with more intensive reading instruction, would she currently be reading on grade level? Explain your response.

_____

_____

_____

_____

_____

_____

_____

4. How should school districts resolve the issue of standards for students with disabilities?

_____

_____

_____

_____

_____

_____

_____

5. Is Marta's school district legally responsible for the tuition for the private learning disabilities school that her parents have selected for next year? Why or why not? What laws might influence this case?

_____

_____

_____

_____

_____

_____

_____

_____

6. Could Marta go on to college when she graduates? Explain your response.

_____

_____

_____

_____

_____

_____

_____

_____

7. How could the school district have handled things differently so that this problem never would have arisen? What could Mr. and Mrs. Martinez have done to prevent this situation?

_____

_____

_____

_____

_____

_____

_____

_____

Mission Heights Senior High

Mission Heights Senior High is a well-established, suburban high school with an excellent academic reputation. In the past year and a half, Mission Heights has slowly begun to integrate students with disabilities into the mainstream. As a result, there has been a great deal of controversy surrounding the decision to move forward with this type of service delivery. The school district is committed to providing students with disabilities an integrated learning environment, but individual schools are encouraged to interpret the term "inclusion" as appropriate to the local need. In this particular school, the principal, Ms. Giovanni, has placed a priority on achieving district standards and most of her efforts are focused here. Issues that are not directly related to the achievement of standards are largely dismissed unless they have the potential to interfere with the scholastic goals of the school.

In a recent faculty meeting, Mission Heights teachers discussed the problem of testing adaptations for special education needs. The faculty was strongly divided on this issue. Some faculty members vehemently stated that there could be no adaptations if Mission Heights were to retain its image as an academically strong school. Discussion of this issue was so vocal and opinionated that Ms. Giovanni decided to appoint a committee to investigate what type of policy should be formulated. In appointing this committee, she made it clear that she didn't really care what the faculty decided to do about this issue, as long as the academic integrity of Mission Heights was retained.

 Case Study Activity

ROLE PLAYING

Break into groups of four or five. Simulate a committee meeting in which the members develop a policy regarding what type of adaptations should be allowed during examinations for students with disabilities. The following roles should be assumed: Mr. Lindsey, Mrs. Goldblatt, Ms. Spungeon, Mr. Reeves, and Ms. Giovanni (an optional role). The simulation should include a discussion exploring the advantages and disadvantages of each type of adaptation. These discussions are to be summarized in writing under the strengths and weaknesses section for each teacher. The discussions do not have to be limited to only those adaptations recommended by each of the teachers included in this committee. Summarize in writing the committee's final recommendation.

TESTING ALTERNATIVES COMMITTEE

Teacher: Mr. Lindsey, algebra

Recommendation: Allow additional time and the use of calculators

Viewpoint: Mr Lindsey doesn't really believe that any testing adaptations should be permitted. He feels that these modifications chip away at the school's long-standing commitment to excellence. These two strategies are offered as a compromise. He feels so strongly about this issue that he is considering leaving Mission Heights after 20 years of service, if the committee becomes too lenient with regard to testing standards.

Strengths	Weaknesses

Teacher: Mrs. Goldblatt, chemistry

Recommendation: Use objective format testing (multiple choice and true/false questions) in place of essay exams

Viewpoint: Mrs. Goldblatt has worked tirelessly to achieve success in her field. She has suffered through many incidents of discrimination and harassment in both her undergraduate and graduate programs of study where there were few women enrolled. She feels that she has had to work three times as hard as most males in her field to achieve the success she currently enjoys as the chair of the chemistry department in a high school that has a national reputation in the area of science. She is immensely proud of her work and her school's reputation. Mrs. Goldblatt believes that increased effort is the key to achieving one's goals, as opposed to implementing adaptations.

Strengths	**Weaknesses**

Teacher: Ms. Spungeon, sociology

Recommendation: Implement a cooperative learning format in which groups of students take the exam together and cooperatively answer the questions; all group members receive the same grade.

Viewpoint: People do their best when they work together for the benefit of the group. Cooperative learning emphasizes group strengths and downplays individual weaknesses. Why should students with disabilities get lower grades on exams if teachers can figure out a way to prevent this from happening? Shouldn't teachers be teaching the merits of interdependency rather than competitiveness for grades? Students with disabilities have enough problems without the increased anxieties of testing.

Strengths	**Weaknesses**

Teacher: Mr. Reeves, special education and life skills

Recommendation: Use open note and open book exams

Viewpoint: For most students with disabilities, taking exams creates such anxiety and stress that they are not able to show all that they know. Memory problems related to test anxiety and cognitive dysfunction interfere with performance, while written expression further complicates the situation. If teachers are truly looking for knowledge on an exam, they should be testing the student for the ability to find the answers in the appropriate resources and to then express these ideas in an oral or written format that is comprehensible. It is grossly unfair to expect students with disabilities to compete with peers who do not experience learning problems.

Strengths	**Weaknesses**

_____   _____

_____   _____

_____   _____

Committee Meeting Summary

_____

_____

_____

_____

_____

_____

_____

_____

_____

_____

_____

_____

_____

_____

_____

_____

_____

_____

_____

_____

_____

_____

_____

_____

_____

_____

Susanne

Susanne is a 5-year-old child who has been identified as having a learning disability. She has been in a noncategorical preschool classroom since the age of 3. The school district would like her to continue in this setting for another year and then go on to kindergarten in her neighborhood school. Susanne's parents, Mr. and Mrs. Devlin, are against this recommendation. They want her to be placed in her neighborhood school with her two older brothers. Mrs. Swanson, Susanne's preschool teacher, feels that the parents don't understand the ramifications of placing Susanne in a kindergarten where she will not be getting one-to-one instruction. Mr. and Mrs. Devlin are active in the Learning Disabilities Association, an organization that encourages parents to advocate for their children with learning disabilities. They have been told that the school district has an obligation to provide Susanne with the education she needs, so it is their perception that this obligation could be met in the neighborhood school just as well as it could be met in her special education setting.

Susanne's current preschool program is associated with a prestigious medical university and child development treatment center. Susanne is provided with physical therapy, occupational therapy, speech–language therapy, and intensive preacademic readiness programming on a daily basis. Her teachers and therapists are highly educated and trained. Mr. and Mrs. Devlin have not been dissatisfied with Susanne's program there, but they have become increasingly uncomfortable with the fact that their daughter's preschool is in a medical school as opposed to being in a neighborhood setting. As they have become more involved with the Learning Disabilities Association, they have listened to parents speak about the pros and cons of segregated settings for their children. They have gradually come to the conclusion that Susanne's social needs should be a priority for her kindergarten year.

The staff at Susanne's school has suggested that it would be a big mistake for Susanne to go to the neighborhood school. They believe that her functioning is so low that her kindergarten teacher will not be able to help her. Mrs. Swanson is very much attached to Susanne. She has worked laboriously with this child to get her to the level at which she is currently functioning. She and her colleagues feel that Susanne will lose all of these hard-won skills if they are not reinforced. Mrs. Swanson feels that if she had one more year to work with Susanne, she could provide an intensive focus on readiness skills that would give her the firm foundation to experience more success in the elementary school years. It is very distressing for her to think that the Devlins could give up Susanne's highly specialized program at the medical school for a public school program.

Background Information:

From an early age, Mrs. Devlin knew that Susanne was not demonstrating normal achievement of developmental milestones. Susanne did not walk or talk until she was almost 2 years of age. When she did begin walking, she seemed to have to concentrate on each step as she moved from point to point. While Susanne's siblings had started showing an interest in coloring at the age of 2, Susanne still couldn't hold a crayon or marker until close to 4. She seemed to have a very difficult time expressing herself. Often she appeared to know what she wanted to say, but the words didn't come out. Instead of using words, she would use sounds to tell family members that she had seen an airplane or a fire truck. Susanne's pediatrician agreed with Mrs. Devlin that Susanne should be provided with a complete developmental evaluation. He referred the family to the medical school.

Susanne's evaluation revealed significant language and visual–motor problems. Although Susanne's receptive language was found to be within the range of normal functioning, her expressive language was 2 years below expectancy. The speech therapist who completed the evaluation told Mr. and Mrs. Devlin that Susanne's language skills were so low that her performance was comparable to that of a child who had been deprived of normal language stimulation, "as if she had been locked in a closet for most of her life." Susanne's motor milestones were so far below expectation, that the psychologist diagnosed her as having "subclinical cerebral palsy," meaning that her motor problems were almost severe enough to meet the criteria for cerebral palsy. Her final diagnosis was that of severe learning disability. The Devlins were devastated when the evaluation team gave the results to them. The team made it clear to the family that Susanne would always have "an uphill battle trying to be like other children." But they also assured the Devlins that through an intensive school program like the one at the medical university, Susanne would be able to make substantial progress. The Devlins signed her up for the program during that same meeting.

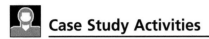 **Case Study Activities**

PART I:
INDIVIDUAL CASE ANALYSIS

Assume the role of a kindergarten teacher and write a two-page narrative explaining how you could meet Susanne's needs in your classroom. Included in this narrative should be a description of: (a) accommodations for language, visual–motor, and social needs, (b) examples of specific strategies for readiness skills, (c) an evaluation system to determine progress, and (d) resources to be used.

PART II:
INDIVIDUAL OR GROUP CASE ANALYSIS

In the space below, provide at least five reasons why Susanne should go to her neighborhood school for kindergarten and another five reasons why she should go back to the special education program at the medical university. Then decide which appears to be the preferable setting and write a paragraph explaining why that particular recommendation seems to be the most appropriate for this child.

Neighborhood School   **Special Education School**

_____   _____

_____   _____

_____   _____

_____   _____

_____   _____

Recommendation

_____

_____

_____

_____

_____

_____

_____

_____

_____

_____

_____

_____

_____

Cognitive and Adaptive Needs

CHAPTER 2

Eli

Eli is a 7-year-old first grader at Green Acres Elementary School. He has Down syndrome. Eli is a quiet, compliant little boy with a pleasant disposition. He is often described as an inactive child. His activity level is so low that he is described as lethargic. Eli also has hypotonia which causes him to appear to be somewhat awkward in fine and gross motor activities. Mrs. Gianetti, his first-grade teacher, is a very warm, loving individual who has welcomed Eli into her class. Of the four first-grade teachers in the building, Mrs. Gianetti was the only teacher who expressed a willingness to have Eli in her classroom. Her attitude is that everyone should be included in the mainstream of life, even though her expectations for Eli are clearly different from those she holds for her other first graders.

Mrs. Gianetti has designed a "cozy corner" exclusively for Eli. In this area, she has placed overstuffed pillows, a quilt, and a variety of preschool picture books. She encourages Eli to spend as much time as he likes in this corner. It is not unusual for him to fall asleep there in the early afternoon and spend 2 hours napping. Mrs. Gianetti spends her own money to buy coloring books for Eli to use in the classroom, which he thoroughly enjoys. She also brings toys (discards from her grandchildren) to school for him to play with. Eli adores Mrs. Gianetti and the affection is returned. Mrs. Gianetti is proud of her inclusion efforts and considers herself to be somewhat of a disability activist because of her acceptance of this child in her classroom.

Background Information:

Eli's parents, Mr. and Mrs. Hamberg, do not want Eli to be in a special education program. They believe that he will do his best if he is challenged in the regular education curriculum. Last year, when the pupil assessment team recommended that Eli be provided with 2½ hours of resource help on a daily basis, they adamantly refused to consider the suggestion or to sign the papers for special education placement. They were delighted when they were informed that there was a first-grade teacher who was willing to have Eli in her classroom. They couldn't have been more pleased when they met Mrs. Gianetti and observed her to be such an accepting and caring individual.

For the first month of the school year, the Hambergs were pleased with Eli's enthusiasm for school, which confirmed their notions regarding the appropriateness of the setting for his needs. They began having second thoughts when Mrs. Hamberg dropped in unexpectedly to bring a rain parka for Eli. Mrs. Hamberg was taken aback when she found Eli in the corner sleeping, while the rest of the class was having math. After that experience, the Hambergs began dropping in frequently. Almost every time they visited, they observed Eli engaged in coloring, playing with toys, or sleeping in his corner. Last week things came to a head when Mrs. Hamberg found Eli sleeping in the corner for the third afternoon in a row. She waited until school was dismissed and then very calmly and firmly explained to Mrs. Gianetti that Eli's curriculum was "totally inappropriate" and would no longer be acceptable. Mrs. Hamberg further stated that from this point forward, she wanted Eli to do whatever the other first graders were doing, and she wanted his "cozy corner" dismantled.

The conference was abruptly terminated when Mrs. Gianetti burst into tears and left for the principal's office. Through a rush of tears, Mrs. Gianetti told the principal that after all she had done for Eli and his family, none of her efforts were appreciated and, in fact, she was being harshly criticized for her hard work.

That same afternoon the principal called an emergency meeting of all the first-grade teachers and asked them to reconsider having Eli placed in one of their classes, since the placement with Mrs. Gianetti wasn't working out. They were vociferous in their defense of Mrs. Gianetti and made remarks to the effect that the parents should be grateful that Mrs. Gianetti even accepted "a child like that" in her class. They were also steadfastly unanimous in their refusal to have Eli moved to one of their classrooms.

 Case Study Activity

INDIVIDUAL OR GROUP CASE ANALYSIS

Answer the following questions and be prepared to discuss them in class.

1. Do Eli's parents have the right to request a different instructional situation given the fact that they have rejected special education services? Why or why not?

_____

_____

_____

_____

_____

_____

_____

_____

_____

2. Are Mrs. Gianetti's feelings justified? Why or why not?

_____

_____

_____

_____

_____

_____

_____

_____

_____

3. Do the other 3 first-grade teachers have a right to reject Eli as one of their students? Why or why not?

_____

_____

_____

_____

_____

_____

_____

_____

4. If you were the principal, what would you do in this situation?

_____

_____

_____

_____

_____

_____

_____

5. Was Eli's curriculum inappropriate for his needs? Why or why not?

_____

_____

_____

_____

_____

_____

_____

6. Are Eli's parents unrealistic about his potential? Why or why not?

_____

_____

_____

_____

_____

_____

_____

7. Could Mr. and Mrs. Hamberg have handled this situation in a different way that might have caused fewer hurtful and angry feelings? What might they have done differently?

_____

_____

_____

_____

_____

_____

_____

_____

Elizabeth

Elizabeth is a 10-year-old child in the third grade at Bennett Elementary School. She has multiple disabilities including cerebral palsy, severe mental retardation, moderate hearing loss, and a seizure disorder. This is Elizabeth's second year in regular education. Last year did not go very well for Elizabeth. Her second-grade teacher showed little interest in including her in academic activities so, for the most part, Elizabeth sat in her chair, waiting for her special education teacher, occupational therapist, or speech therapist to come and get her. The special education staff had wanted to provide therapy for Elizabeth in the second-grade classroom, but the teacher declined, saying that it was too distracting for the other students. Elizabeth's teacher this year, Mrs. Gables, is determined that Elizabeth is going to be an active member of the class. She hasn't had any experience with children like Elizabeth, so she has

asked Mrs. Jennings, the special education teacher, to help her.

Elizabeth relies on the use of a wheelchair because she has paraplegia as a result of the cerebral palsy. Although she can use her arms, her movements are characterized by spasticity. Mrs. Gables feels that Elizabeth should be using a desk like the other children in the classroom, but she doesn't know if she should be moving her in and out of the wheelchair like that. When Mrs. Gables brought this up to Elizabeth's mother, Mrs. Valle, she was told that Elizabeth would be fine in her chair. Her mother said that Mrs. Gables didn't need to be straining her back by moving Elizabeth in and out of her desk because it didn't matter to Elizabeth where she sat.

Mrs. Gables has also mentioned to Mrs. Valle that Elizabeth asks for food during lunch, and she wonders if she is getting enough to eat. Elizabeth is tube fed by the school nurse prior to going to the cafeteria. It bothers Mrs. Gables that Elizabeth just sits there looking hungry while the other children are eating. Again, Mrs. Valle told her not to worry. She said that Elizabeth would eat all day if she were allowed, and that her tube feeding provided her with all the nourishment she needed. She also said that Elizabeth would have food all over herself, and the other kids would have a field day teasing her if she started eating in the cafeteria. Mrs. Gables doesn't have the impression that Mrs. Valle is really interested in having Elizabeth participate during lunch. Sometimes she feels that Elizabeth's mother doesn't really care about Elizabeth's curriculum at school. She doesn't like to be critical of parents with children like Elizabeth, but she can't help feeling that something is not right with this parent–child relationship.

Mrs. Gables is planning a unit on transportation, and she would like Elizabeth to be able to participate. She has asked Mrs. Jennings to come into her room and work with her on this unit, so that she can better understand what adaptations and modifications Elizabeth needs. Mrs. Jennings said that she would be delighted to work with Mrs. Gables on "curriculum overlapping" for the transportation unit. Mrs. Jennings explained to Mrs. Gables that this is a technique whereby the content is examined to determine how it can be modified for students who are working on other objectives. Mrs. Jennings is currently working on number concepts, range of motion, and vocabulary with Elizabeth. She mentioned to Mrs. Gables that this transportation unit would be an ideal place to start because the content would probably be motivating to Elizabeth as her father is an airline pilot. Mrs. Gables is glad that Mrs. Jennings will be working closely with her because she has no idea where to start teaching Elizabeth.

Background Information:

Elizabeth was adopted when she was 2 days old by Mr. and Mrs. Valle, who had tried for years to have children of their own. During the first 6 months of life, it became obvious to the Valles that Elizabeth was not developing as expected. However, they did not find out the full extent of her disabilities until she was almost 2. Mrs. Valle became deeply depressed when she came to the realization that Elizabeth would never walk and would be severely mentally retarded with limited communication skills. At that time, she told her husband that she wanted to give Elizabeth back to the adoption agency, but he would not hear of it. Mr. Valle wanted to adopt another child, but Mrs. Valle would not agree unless Elizabeth were relinquished. This disagreement became a major point of contention that was never resolved.

After Elizabeth was diagnosed as having multiple disabilities, Mrs. Valle hired a full-time, live-in nanny to care for Elizabeth because she did not feel that she was able to do this. Mr. Valle became immersed in his work and signed on for more international flights, which resulted in him spending less and less time at home. Mrs. Valle began spending less time with her daughter and started taking up a variety of hobbies and volunteer work that kept her very busy. Last year, Mrs. Valle had an apartment added on to their house. She moved the nanny and Elizabeth into this addition. Since the parents have not told the nanny what kinds of activities they would like her to involve Elizabeth in, the two of them spend most of their time in front of the television.

Although Elizabeth has the physical abilities to mouth feed, her mother told the nanny that she finds it more convenient and less messy to use the tube feeding procedure. The occupational therapist at Bennett Elementary School has offered to start feeding Elizebeth food during lunch so she can feel like she's participating more, but Mrs. Valle did not seem too happy with this idea. She told the therapist that she doubted very much if Elizabeth cared one way or the other. The therapist decided not to pursue it at the time because of Mrs. Valle's attitude, but she's definitely going to bring it up again at the annual review.

Case Study Activity

INDIVIDUAL OR GROUP CASE ANALYSIS

Answer the following questions and be prepared to discuss them in class.

1. Is there any way that the school can work with this family to get them more involved in this child's life? Describe three strategies you might use if you were Mrs. Gables.

_____

_____

_____

_____

_____

_____

_____

_____

2. Do you think that Elizabeth should be eating food in the cafeteria with the other students at lunchtime? Why might this be important for Elizabeth? Do you think that Mrs. Valle's concerns about teasing are valid?

_____

_____

_____

_____

_____

_____

_____

_____

3. Do you think that the goal of transference from the wheelchair to the desk might be an appropriate one for this child? Why or why not? Why do you think that Mrs. Valle is not interested in this goal?

_____

_____

_____

_____

_____

_____

_____

_____

4. Explain how Mrs. Jennings and Mrs. Gables could teach number concepts and vocabulary, as well as increase range of motion during the upcoming transportation unit? Develop a sample transportation lesson from this unit, and explain how it can be modified to address these three skills for Elizabeth.

_____

_____

_____

_____

_____

_____

_____

_____

5. If you were Mrs. Gables, would you ask Mr. Valle to become involved in the transportation unit? Why or why not? In what way might he be able to participate? How could this help Elizabeth?

_____

_____

_____

_____

_____

_____

_____

6. If you were Elizabeth's teachers, would you allow her to have speech therapy and occupational therapy in class, or would you ask that she be taken out for this assistance?

_____

_____

_____

_____

_____

_____

_____

_____

_____

7. How might parenting a child with a disability impact a couple's marital relationship? Give specific examples of difficulties that may be confronted.

_____

_____

_____

_____

_____

_____

_____

_____

_____

_____

_____

Geraldo

Geraldo is a 13-year-old seventh grader at Hilltop Middle School. He has been identified as having mild mental retardation. During the elementary school years, he was placed in a self-contained classroom. Geraldo is currently integrated in all regular education classes. Hilltop Middle School is committed to providing inclusive environments for all students with disabilities and does not have any special class placements. Although most of Hilltop's teachers are receptive to this general philosophy of mainstreaming, they are concerned by a number of implementation issues with which they have not previously dealt. One of these issues involves how Geraldo is to be graded. There are many different opinions on the appropriateness of various evaluation methods. The principal, Mr. Ritter, has basically left the matter in the hands of the teachers. He feels that resolving this difficulty will help make these teachers more invested in successful integration. Mr. Ritter has asked Geraldo's teachers to work together as a committee and make a decision regarding the most appropriate means of grading this student.

Background Information:

Geraldo was staffed into a self-contained class for students with disabilities during kindergarten. His grades have consistently been high due to the amount of effort he puts forth in his schoolwork. During the primary years he received S+ for all subject areas. When he was in the intermediate grades, he received As and Bs for his work. Geraldo is the type of student who is very conscientious about school. He has missed only one day since he started. His special education teachers have all been impressed with his excellent work habits and positive attitude toward school.

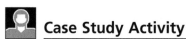 **Case Study Activity**

ROLE PLAYING

Break into groups of four or five and assume one of the following roles: Mrs. Sims, Mr. Georges, Ms. Shieh, Mr. Flanders, and Mr. Ritter (an optional role). Simulate a meeting in which these teachers attempt to reach a consensus regarding the best means to evaluate Geraldo. Be sure to discuss the advantages and disadvantages of each grading system and summarize these in writing under the strengths and weaknesses section. Grading options other than those described should also be considered. Following the role-playing activity, provide a final written recommendation for grading students with disabilities.

Grading Alternatives Committee

Mrs. Sims, math teacher

Recommendation: Use the traditional grading method

Viewpoint: Geraldo is in the regular education system, so his teachers can assume that he is capable of keeping up with his peers.

Strengths	**Weaknesses**
_____	_____
_____	_____
_____	_____
_____	_____

Mr. Georges, social studies teacher

Recommendation: Use a pass/fail approach

Viewpoint: Geraldo is part of his class just like the other students. He should be given a "fair shot" at doing the work that everyone else is doing without the pressure of getting bad grades or comparing himself to peers who are getting As.

Strengths	**Weaknesses**
_____	_____
_____	_____
_____	_____
_____	_____

Ms. Shieh, English teacher

Recommendation: Use ungraded evaluations

Viewpoint: This student is retarded. There's no way I can grade his work. How can he possibly fulfill middle school English requirements such as expository writing. Give him a break!

Strengths	**Weaknesses**
_____	_____
_____	_____

_____   _____

_____   _____

Mr. Flanders, special education teacher

Recommendation: Base evaluations upon IEP goals and objectives

Viewpoint: Geraldo should not be evaluated in reference to peer progress. He should be evaluated in reference to the specific goals and objectives contained in the IEP; otherwise, what's the purpose of that document?

Strengths	**Weaknesses**
_____	_____
_____	_____
_____	_____
_____	_____

Committee Meeting Summary

_____

_____

_____

_____

_____

_____

_____

_____

_____

_____

_____

_____

_____

_____

_____

_____

_____

Hwa-Fang

Hwa-Fang is a 9-year-old student at Canalside Elementary. She has recently begun second grade in Mrs. London's class. Mrs. London has been told that Hwa-Fang is probably mentally retarded and that she has an expressive vocabulary of approximately only 10 words. She also has mild spastic cerebral palsy and seizures that are mostly controlled with the help of phenobarbital. Hwa-Fang was evaluated last year in kindergarten. The results of this evaluation revealed that her IQ was 60. Adaptive skills, as measured by the Vineland Adaptive Behavior Scales, were found to be significantly below age level. It was recommended that Hwa-Fang be placed in a full-time special education class, which would concentrate on teaching her English and remediating the areas of weakness that had been identified by this evaluation. Mr. and Mrs. Epstein, Hwa-Fang's parents, disagreed with the evaluation and refused the special education placement. They want her in the regular classroom and are willing to hire professionals on a private basis to provide her with speech–language therapy, occupational–physical therapy, and academic remediation outside of school.

Background Information:

Hwa-Fang was born in a remote, rural area of China. Her biological parents abandoned her on the steps of an American missionary's home. Hwa-Fang was taken to an orphanage in Beijing and lived there for 8 years. She was not adopted because of her cerebral palsy. At the age of 8, the missionary family who originally cared for her arranged for an adoption of Hwa-Fang by a well-to-do family in the United States.

Hwa-Fang's adoptive parents are both attorneys in their late forties. They have no other children. Both Mr. and Mrs. Epstein are active in their community. Mrs. Epstein is employed by the American Civil Liberties Union and contributes a great deal of volunteer time to Amnesty International. Mr. Epstein works for the state immigration and naturalization agency and contributes many hours of community service to the Jewish Anti-Defamation League. The Epsteins are committed to giving this child the best opportunities this country has to offer.

Mr. and Mrs. Epstein welcomed the special education evaluation that was recommended when Hwa-Fang entered school at Canalside. They looked forward to the staffing where they were to hear the results of Hwa-Fang's testing. However, they were bitterly disappointed with the results. Their main contention is that Hwa-Fang does not know enough English to have her intelligence tested. It made no difference to them when they were told that a nonverbal intelligence test was used with Hwa-Fang. They were incredulous that a child with cerebral palsy was tested by a measure largely dependent upon visual–motor proficiency. Mr. and Mrs. Epstein were outraged that professionals would use such inappropriate measurement techniques to come up with a prejudiced diagnosis of mental retardation. They see this assessment as an attempt to pigeonhole their child into a low-achieving track where she will not receive the necessary stimulation to spur achievement. In no uncertain terms, they let the school know that they would not allow Hwa-Fang to receive any special services during the school day, and any further attempt to label her as mentally retarded would result in litigation.

 ## Case Study Activity

INDIVIDUAL OR GROUP CASE ANALYSIS

Answer the following questions and be prepared to discuss them in class.

1. Was the school system right in their attempt to assess Hwa-Fang's intelligence with these tests? Why or why not? What other testing alternatives would be available for use with a child like Hwa-Fang?

_____

_____

_____

_____

_____

_____

_____

2. Do you support the parents' position to withhold special education services during the school day? Why or why not?

_____

_____

_____

_____

_____

_____

_____

3. If you were Hwa-Fang's teacher, how would you attempt to increase her English skills within your language arts program?

_____

_____

_____

_____

_____

_____

4. If you were Hwa-Fang's teacher, how would you work with her family to increase the effectiveness of your classroom instruction?

_____

_____

_____

_____

_____

_____

_____

5. Do you think Hwa-Fang's diagnosis of mental retardation is biased? Is there any other explanation for her low performance on the test of adaptive behavior?

_____

_____

_____

_____

_____

_____

6. Is an IQ test that focuses on visual–motor performance an appropriate choice for this child? Why or why not?

_____

_____

_____

_____

_____

_____

_____

Keisha

Keisha is a 9-year-old third grader at Walnut Grove Elementary. She has Down syndrome and has been in a self-contained special education placement since the age of 3. Her parents, Mr. and Mrs. Labonne, have been very pleased with their daughter's school program. Keisha has had only two special education teachers during the past 5 years. Both of these teachers have been highly energetic, very knowledgeable in diagnostic–prescriptive teaching strategies, and skilled in collaborating with parents and other teachers. Walnut Grove is currently in the process of shifting to a district-wide inclusion program and has recommended that Keisha discontinue her special class in favor of integration into a regular third-grade classroom. The principal, Mrs. Taylor, has been told that there will be no special education class at Walnut Grove. This program will be replaced by a part-time teacher who will consult with regular educators on behalf of the students with identified disabilities.

Background Information:

When Keisha was born, Mr. and Mrs. Labonne were provided with a rather grim prognosis for their daughter. The pediatrician informed them that it was likely that Keisha would have severe mental retardation and a myriad of health problems, such as a cardiac defect and ongoing respiratory illness. This pediatrician also suggested that it would be unlikely that this child would ever be toilet trained or able to care for herself. He recommended that the Labonnes consider arranging for a foster care situation rather than attempting to raise her in their home. Although the Labonnes were devastated by Keisha's birth defect, they were horrified by their doctor's suggestion that this child would be better off in another family's care. They promptly changed pediatricians and began taking Keisha to a doctor who was much more accepting of her disability.

Although Keisha did have three heart operations and currently has respiratory problems requiring the daily use of oxygen, she has developed much more quickly than anyone could have imagined. She was completely toilet trained by the age of 4 and, by the age of 5, she was able to dress herself and brush her teeth without the least assistance from her parents. Keisha is an engaging child with a pleasant disposition and a marvelous sense of humor. Everyone who knows Keisha agrees that her strengths far outnumber her weaknesses.

Mr. and Mrs. Labonne have worked tirelessly with Keisha to achieve her current level of self-care and social skill proficiency. However, they generally credit Keisha's special education teachers, Mrs. Christiansen and Mr. Guerrari, with her preacademic and academic achievement. Mr. and Mrs. Labonne are seriously troubled over the prospect of their daughter losing the protective and nurturing environment that her special education teachers have provided. They are also fearful that Keisha will be ridiculed by the other children in the mainstream. Their biggest concern, however, is that Keisha will start to lose the ground that has been so laboriously gained in special education. They can see few, if any, benefits to this so-called integration, particularly since the regular third-grade teacher that Keisha will have has admitted that she "has no idea how to teach Keisha," even though she is "looking forward to having her in the classroom." When the Labonne's compare the prospect of this type of curriculum with the intensive one-to-one instruction that has brought Keisha close to the point of reading, they become frustrated and depressed.

Mr. Guerrari, her special education teacher for the last 2 years, is not a supporter of the movement toward inclusion in the schools. It is his opinion that most children with disabilities can make far greater progress in a special education classroom with a teacher specifically trained to meet the needs of these children. He's also not looking forward to his new position in which he will be split between three different schools.

Mr. and Mrs. Labonne have requested a meeting with Mrs. Taylor and Mr. Guerrari to discuss this impending change in placement. They have already informed Mrs. Taylor that they are familiar with special education law, especially the part that states schools must offer an array of placement services for students with disabilities. They have also indicated that they intend to pursue their rights through whatever means are necessary to secure the most appropriate placement for their daughter. This conversation made Mrs. Taylor nervous enough that she decided to ask the special director of Summerton School District, Mr. Busby, to join the meeting. Mr. Busby is a strong advocate for inclusion. He has a brother with Down syndrome who spent 10 years in a state institution on the advice of the family physician. He is somewhat bitter that the family received such bad advice and that his brother had to spend so much of his childhood at the residential facility before the family came to terms with the disability and took the child home. Mr. Busby is pleased to be invited to meetings that provide him the opportunity to advocate for inclusive environments. He fought long and hard to get the school district to agree to this move to full inclusion.

 Case Study Activities

PART I:
ROLE PLAYING

Break into groups of four or five. Simulate a conference in which the family and the school representatives discuss how to resolve this problem. The following roles should be assumed by group members: Mr. Labonne, Mr. Guerrari, Mrs. Taylor, Mr. Busby, and Mrs. Labonne (an optional role). Provide a written summary of the group's resolution.

Resolution

_____

_____

_____

_____

_____

_____

_____

_____

_____

PART II:
INDIVIDUAL OR GROUP CASE ANALYSIS

Give five reasons why each of the following parties has a valid argument for their position regarding Keisha's placement. After examining these reasons, provide your own recommendation for Keisha's placement and the resolution of this problem.

1. Mr. and Mrs. Labonne:

_____

_____

_____

_____

_____

_____

2. Mr. Guerrari:

_____

_____

_____

_____

_____

_____

_____

_____

3. Mr. Busby:

_____

_____

_____

_____

_____

_____

_____

Recommendation for Placement

_____

_____

_____

_____

_____

_____

_____

_____

_____

_____

_____

_____

_____

_____

_____

_____

_____

_____

Lemar

Lemar is a 6-year-old kindergarten student at Pine Knolls Elementary. He was diagnosed with Fragile X syndrome at the age of 2. He has spent the last 3 years in a noncategorical, special education preschool setting. This will be his first year in a regular education classroom. Lemar has the prominent physical characteristics associated with Fragile X, such as large ears, broad forehead, and a long narrow face. His most recent evaluation indicates mild mental retardation. Lemar's behavioral characteristics include short attention span and autistic-like actions such as hand flapping, toe walking, and poor eye contact. In addition to these difficulties, Lemar is hypersensitive to touch, smell, taste, and hearing. He also engages in self-injurious behavior, particularly hand biting. It is not unusual for him to draw blood if he is not carefully monitored. While Mrs. Swiderski, his kindergarten teacher, is not exactly thrilled with the prospect of having Lemar in her class, she is a committed teacher who takes her responsibilities seriously. The principal has arranged to have an aide with Lemar for 1 hour of the 2½-hour kindergarten day.

Background Information:

Lemar has an 11-year-old brother, Andre, who also has Fragile X syndrome. Andre was institutionalized last year because of behavioral problems including vandalism, stealing, and truancy. Andre's difficulties escalated at the age of 7. When he was being evaluated at that time, the school psychologist noted that baby Lemar shared the same physical features associated with Fragile X. He recommended that their mother, Mrs. Prutch, have Lemar tested. Lemar was evaluated through Child Find and diagnosed with the same genetic disorder. The major difference between the

brothers is that Andre has learning disabilities whereas Lemar has mental retardation. Andre is also hypersensitive, and it is this sensitivity to stimulation that results in his violent outbursts of temper. Andre's behavioral incidents are usually triggered by touching, pushing, or teasing.

Mrs. Prutch is a single parent with limited resources. She supports her family through welfare, as the father abandoned the family shortly after Lemar's birth. While Mrs. Prutch apparently provides for Lemar's physical needs, she appears to have limited energy for other parenting responsibilities.

Lemar's preschool years were somewhat problematic because of his behavior. His hypersensitivity caused him to respond adversely to smells from the cafeteria, normal sounds from the building, and any type of visual distraction. For example, if certain strong odors, such as those from pizza or tacos, drifted up to the classroom, Lemar would react by holding his nose, screaming, and rolling around on the floor. Similar behaviors were demonstrated when the public address system was used or when the bell rang. In addition to these behaviors, his self-abusive hand biting was a constant source of concern for his teachers. Whenever they tried to enlist the help of Mrs. Prutch in a behavior management program, she would fail to show up for meetings or return their phone calls. In the special education setting of 11 students, a teacher, and an aide, it was all the staff could do to keep Lemar from seriously injuring himself. His special education teacher recommended that he be placed in a self-contained special needs kindergarten. The school district did not follow this recommendation as they have recently adopted a policy of inclusion for all students with disabilities who have the potential to benefit from the regular education environment.

 ## Case Study Activity

INDIVIDUAL OR GROUP CASE ANALYSIS

Answer the following questions and be prepared to discuss them in class.

1. What resources can Mrs. Swiderski use to prepare herself to work with Lemar? Name at least two different resources, and explain why these might be useful.

_____

_____

_____

_____

_____

2. What can Mrs. Swiderski do in her classroom to help Lemar with his hypersensitivity? Give four specific suggestions.

_____

_____

_____

_____

_____

_____

_____

3. What type of behavior management plan could Mrs. Swiderski implement to decrease Lemar's hand biting?

_____

_____

_____

_____

_____

_____

_____

4. How can Mrs. Swiderski determine Lemar's strengths? How might she use this information in her planning?

_____

_____

_____

_____

_____

_____

_____

5. Is the regular classroom an appropriate placement for Lemar? Why or why not? Give at least three reasons for your opinion.

_____

_____

_____

_____

_____

_____

6. Do you think that Lemar will eventually be placed in a residential facility like his brother, Andre? How could his chances for successful school and community integration be increased?

_____

_____

_____

_____

_____

_____

7. List four possible reasons why Mrs. Prutch has not been involved in Lemar's educational planning thus far. If you were Mrs. Swiderski, how would you attempt to establish and sustain communication with this parent?

_____

_____

_____

_____

_____

_____

Peter

Peter is a 15-year-old student at Andrew Jackson High School. Peter has mental retardation that falls into the severe to profound range of functioning. He also uses a wheelchair because of spastic cerebral palsy, which has affected all four limbs. Peter is not able to use his arms or hands, but he has some very limited movement in his right leg. Peter is nonverbal; that is, he is not able to use signs or a computerized communication board because of his severe cognitive and physical disabilities. However, this student seems to genuinely enjoy being around his peers. Peter smiles a great deal when there are a lot of students around him. He enjoys being touched, and he likes all kinds of music.

This is Peter's second year at Andrew Jackson High. Last year he was in the GOALS program, a special education placement designed to teach life skills to students with disabilities. This year his mother, Mrs. Dawkins, has asked that Peter be changed to the regular education program. She is appalled by the lack of educational benefit that her son experienced last year. The GOALS program was basically designed for students who have the potential to move into a semi-independent living situation or an assisted employment placement. Since Peter is never going to have these opportunities, Mrs. Dawkins thinks that it is a waste of his time to be in this program. She feels that he does not have the communication or physical skills to benefit from this placement. These classes are small and very quiet. Peter's mother feels they are lacking in the stimulation that Peter needs. He usually just sits in his wheelchair and watches the other students as they learn to read bus schedules and menus. Mrs. Dawkins never wanted Peter in this program, but the principal, Mrs. McVickers, urged her to give it a try. Mrs. McVickers told her that it would give Peter the opportunity to learn how to be part of the "real world of community living." This year Mrs. Dawkins went back to the principal and told her that she had given GOALS a chance and, since it didn't work for her son, she wanted him placed in the "real world of school."

Mrs. McVickers is perplexed by Mrs. Dawkins' request, but she knows that Mrs. Dawkins is serious about this placement change and she wants to be sensitive to this mother's concerns. Mrs. McVickers cannot imagine how Peter could benefit from the regular high school curriculum. She does not believe that this is where Peter should be, but she also knows that Mrs. Dawkins will go to the assistant superintendent to resolve this situation if she doesn't take care of it now. She has decided to organize a committee of faculty members to tackle this problem. Mrs. McVickers plans to ask this faculty committee to determine how Peter could be integrated into each of their classes. She carefully chose four faculty members, whom she knows to be generous of spirit, fair-minded, patient, and hard working.

Background Information:

Peter has been included in the regular education school program since the third grade. This particular school district has been known to be one of the most progressive in terms of implementing some of the earliest inclusion programs. Mrs. Dawkins has always felt that Peter has benefited enormously from the stimulation of peers who do not have disabilities. One of her best memories is of the time she was called to Peter's elementary school to meet his Circle of Friends. She does not believe in segregation, and she doesn't understand why such a progressive school system would go backwards at the secondary level when they had done such a good job at the elementary and middle school levels. She is determined that Peter is going to have the most stimulating learning environment possible and, if the school does not change the special education placement, she will pursue the matter through legal channels. She has already contacted the Association for Community Living, which recommended an attorney for Peter if the need arises.

 ## Case Study Activities

PART I:
ROLE PLAYING

Break into groups of four or five. Simulate a meeting of the faculty members in which this inclusion problem is resolved. The following teachers' roles should be assumed: Mr. Herrold (algebra), Mrs. Scoggins (English), Ms. Bastilla (Spanish), Mr. Wong (history), and Mrs. McVickers (an optional role). Mrs. McVickers has asked the group to develop a plan whereby Peter could be successfully integrated into their classes at Andrew Jackson High. This kind of integration has never been attempted at this school before. The GOALS program is known as a model program for students with disabilities, and parents are usually quite happy to have their students there. In this role-playing activity, Mrs. McVickers will have just finished summarizing what Mrs. Dawkins wants for Peter. She has asked these teachers how they might be able to accomplish such a plan of integration given this student's level of functioning. Their initial response will be one of shock and skepticism. Following the role-playing activity, provide a written summary of each teacher's inclusion accommodations for Peter.

Accommodations

Mr. Herrold

_____

_____

_____

_____

_____

Mrs. Scoggins

_____

_____

_____

_____

_____

Ms. Bastilla

_____

_____

_____

_____

_____

Mr. Wong

_____

_____

_____

_____

PART II:
INDIVIDUAL OR GROUP CASE ANALYSIS

Answer the following questions and be prepared to discuss them in class.

1. Do you agree or disagree with Mrs. Dawkin's request for regular classroom placement for Peter? Explain your response.

_____

_____

_____

_____

_____

_____

_____

2. Why do you think that Mrs. Dawkins believes the regular classroom environment would be more stimulating for her son?

_____

_____

_____

_____

_____

_____

_____

3. In general, do you feel that it is easier to integrate a student with a disability in the elementary and middle school years than it is to accomplish this at the secondary level? Why or why not?

_____

_____

_____

_____

_____

_____

_____

4. What is a Circle of Friends? Could this socialization method be used effectively at the secondary level? Support your response.

_____

_____

_____

_____

_____

_____

_____

_____

5. What is the Association for Community Living? Why would Mrs. Dawkins contact such an organization? What types of services does this organization provide?

_____

_____

_____

_____

_____

_____

_____

_____

6. What does the term _normalization_ refer to? What is the relationship between normalization and inclusion?

_____

_____

_____

_____

_____

_____

_____

_____

7. What laws might influence this case if one or both parties chose to pursue it in court? Are there any precedents for this educational placement question?

_____

_____

_____

_____

_____

_____

_____

_____

_____

_____

_____

Sammy

Sammy is an 8-year-old first-grade student at River Ridge Elementary. His teacher, Mrs. Lopez, is having a very difficult time integrating this child into her class of 25 students. He has been diagnosed as mildly mentally retarded with accompanying attention-deficit/hyperactivity disorder. He receives special education support services for 1 hour each morning and spends the remaining time in the first-grade classroom. Academically, he is working on a readiness level in reading and math. His fine motor skills are quite poor, and he cannot write his name or numbers legibly. Although these academic difficulties are of concern to Mrs. Lopez, it is Sammy's behavior that is more pressing at this point. This child is extremely impulsive. He cannot seem to stay seated for more than 2 or 3 minutes without supervision. He is also very aggressive and frequently hits, pushes, and kicks the other children with only the slightest provocation. He has no friends and doesn't seem to understand how to play or work with others. In spite of these problems, Sammy demonstrates a real interest in learning when he is able to attend to instructional material. It is not unusual for him to bring a book over to Mrs. Lopez and ask her to help him read or to tell her that he has learned a new word. Mrs. Lopez feels that he has untapped potential, but she is concerned that it will take years to make significant progress unless his behavior can be managed more effectively.

Background Information:

Sammy was held back in kindergarten because of concerns regarding his development. He was referred for special education evaluation at the beginning of this year. In addition to his mental retardation, attentional deficits, and hyperactivity, he displays characteristics that indicate he may have fetal alcohol syndrome. This could not be confirmed because Sammy's father, Mr. Ferrer, would not take him to see a pediatrician. The pupil assessment team could not get Mr. Ferrer to participate in the evaluation.

Mrs. Lopez has also tried to get Mr. Ferrer involved with Sammy's school problems, but she has had little cooperation. Sammy's previous teachers have expressed concern and frustration about this child's family situation. He lives with his father who will not supply any information about Sammy's mother. She apparently left the family shortly after Sammy was born and has no contact with him. Sammy is consistently dirty and often wears ripped clothing (his peers report that he usually doesn't wear underwear). He has no siblings, and teachers have the impression that he is often left alone by his father. When Mr. Ferrer has been asked to come to school for conferences, he almost always declines, saying that he can't miss work. The one time he did come to school was when he signed the papers for Sammy's special education placement. On that occasion, when asked if he would be willing to participate in a behavior management program that involved a home–school behavior notebook, he declined saying, "I don't want you to go to any extra trouble for him, he just ain't worth it." When the school personnel protested the remark, Mr. Ferrer quickly left.

 ## Case Study Activity

INDIVIDUAL OR GROUP CASE ANALYSIS

Answer the following questions and be prepared to discuss them in class.

1. How could Mrs. Lopez motivate Mr. Ferrer to come to school to discuss Sammy's progress? Give four possible strategies she might use.

   _____

   _____

   _____

   _____

   _____

   _____

   _____

2. Does Sammy's current living situation constitute abuse or neglect? Why or why not? What can Mrs. Lopez do about Sammy's home life?

   _____

   _____

   _____

   _____

   _____

   _____

3. What type of reading program might be the most effective for Sammy? Why?

   _____

   _____

   _____

_____

_____

_____

_____

4. Should Mrs. Lopez ask the school nurse to refer this child for a fetal alcohol syndrome evaluation? Why or why not? Describe the characteristics of this syndrome.

_____

_____

_____

_____

_____

_____

_____

5. What kinds of strategies could Mrs. Lopez use to increase Sammy's attention span? Give four examples.

_____

_____

_____

_____

_____

_____

6. What kinds of strategies could Mrs. Lopez use to decrease Sammy's impulsivity and aggressive behavior?

_____

_____

_____

_____

_____

7. What is the prognosis for a child like Sammy? Do you think that a teacher can make a difference for a child such as this? Explain your answer.

_____

_____

_____

_____

_____

_____

Vincent

Vincent is an 18-year-old senior at Lincoln High School. He was diagnosed as mildly mentally retarded when he was in the first grade. Since this time, he has been in self-contained special education classrooms for all instruction except for physical education, music, and art. In a couple of months, he will graduate and begin a job with a local pizza restaurant chain. He has received job preparation training through a life skills program at Lincoln.

For the past year, Vincent has been complaining to his parents, Mr. and Mrs. Mancuso, that he doesn't want to go to work for Pizza Prince when he finishes school. He says he's sick of pizza and wants to get a job working on the assembly line of a local auto manufacturer. Mrs. Mancuso has spoken to Mr. Keating, Vincent's special education teacher, who says it simply would not be possible for Vincent to hold that type of employment. Although Mr. Keating did not come right out and say it, Mrs. Mancuso got the definite impression that he felt Vincent was lucky that Pizza Prince had offered him a job at competitive pay, that is, minimum wage. Most of Mr. Keating's students in the life skills program are paid much less than that.

When Mrs. Mancuso told Vincent that he had no other choice but to take this job, Vincent got very angry and told his parents he was going to drop out of school and spend the next few months looking for another kind of job. This distressed both Mr. and Mrs.

Mancuso. They are looking forward to Vincent graduating with a high school diploma, an accomplishment that neither of them were able to attain.

Background Information:

When Vincent was originally diagnosed as mentally retarded, his IQ was determined to be 62 on the full scale of the _Wechsler Intelligence Scale for Children–Revised_ (WISC–R; Wechsler, 1974), with a performance scale of 67 and a verbal scale of 57. Vincent had a very difficult time with language processing and was originally referred for evaluation because of suspected problems with language comprehension. It was determined that Vincent would probably have a better opportunity for learning in a self-contained classroom where the teacher could help him with his language difficulties on a one-to-one or small-group basis. Vincent enjoyed his elementary and middle school years. He spoke positively of his special education teachers and appeared to enjoy socializing with his classmates. He did not see his classmates over the weekend because they lived in different neighborhoods, so he was always eager to return to school on Monday morning.

His high school years did not go as well for Vincent. The friends he had made in elementary and middle school went to a different high school. The students that were in his life skills classroom were, for the most part, lower functioning than Vincent. He soon found that he had nothing in common with most of them. Mr. and Mrs. Mancuso were surprised and upset when they discovered that Vincent was no longer in a classroom with students who were similar to him, but Mr. Keating explained that Vincent could be given a more appropriate education for his needs along with the individualized attention for his language problems in a classroom such as this. Out of the eight students in this classroom, three were autistic, two were severely retarded, and two were moderately retarded. Vincent was the only student who was functioning in the mild range of mental retardation. Mr. Keating told the Mancusos that if Vincent stayed in this program, he could assure them that he would receive a high school diploma, but if he were in the mainstream he wasn't sure that would happen. Mr. Keating felt that the demands of the regular classroom would be such that Vincent would become discouraged and drop out. He also told them that if Vincent stayed in his program, he could almost guarantee them that Vincent would be gainfully employed by the time he left high school. Even though Mr. and Mrs. Mancuso continued to worry about Vincent's unhappiness, they felt he must stay in Mr. Keating's program for his own benefit.

The major objective of the life skills program at Lincoln is to find an appropriate vocational area for each student and to assist with the development of transition skills to help the student move from school to community life. Mr. Keating's program provided the students with two different employment options—food service and janitorial. Two major companies con-tracted with Lincoln so that life skills class graduates would be guaranteed jobs when they left school. Mr. Keating conducts an extensive potential profile of each of his students before they are placed in either janitor-ial or food service. However, that was not the case with Vincent, as he informed Mr. Keating on the first day of class that, "I ain't going to be no janitor." Mr. Keating felt that all students deserved flexibility whenever it could be provided, so he placed Vincent in the food service program with the autistic and severely retarded students.

Although Vincent never liked the Pizza Prince program, he didn't really talk too much about it. In fact, during his high school years, he became distant and didn't interact with his parents or friends as he had in years before. Mr. and Mrs. Mancuso felt that he was just going through a stage, so they didn't worry too much. They were grateful that he didn't get into trou-ble like many of their friends' teenagers. But now that he has talked about dropping out, they are very upset. They are frustrated by Mr. Keating, but they are afraid to say anything more to him. They can't understand why working at a pizza restaurant is the only job that their son can hold.

Mr. Keating is feeling frustrated about Vincent and his family as well. He has spent a great deal of time with this student, and he feels very proud that Vincent will be employed on a competitive basis. He is also very proud of his life skills class, which is considered to be a model program in this city. It bothers him that instead of thanking him, the Mancusos seem to be indirectly criticizing him. He really doesn't understand what they expect.

 ## Case Study Activity

INDIVIDUAL OR GROUP CASE ANALYSIS

Answer the following questions and be prepared to discuss them in class.

1. Do you think Vincent is at risk for dropping out of school? Why or why not?

_____

_____

_____

_____

_____

_____

_____

_____

_____

_____

2. Explain Mr. Keating's position on vocational training for students with disabilities. Why does he feel that Vincent and his family should be grateful for his efforts? Do you agree? Why or why not?

_____

_____

_____

_____

_____

_____

_____

_____

_____

3. Should a student like Vincent have other options in addition to janitorial and food service? Should the teacher and school district be expected to develop vocational programs for all types of opportunities? Why or why not?

_____

_____

_____

_____

_____

_____

_____

_____

_____

4. In addition to disliking food service, is there another reason why Vincent doesn't like this vocational program? What modifications could be made to alleviate this problem?

_____

_____

_____

_____

_____

_____

_____

_____

_____

_____

5. If you were Vincent's parents, what would you do about this situation?

_____

_____

_____

_____

_____

_____

_____

_____

_____

_____

_____

_____

_____

6. What is the possibility that an individual like Vincent could be trained for a job in auto manufacturing? Support your answer.

_____

_____

_____

_____

_____

_____

_____

_____

_____

_____

_____

_____

_____

7. Is competitive employment the most important criteria for job training? Would it make sense for an individual to earn less in a job that he preferred? Explain your answer.

_____

_____

_____

_____

_____

_____

_____

_____

_____

8. How could the school work with this student and his family to resolve this problem?

_____

_____

_____

_____

Attentional Needs

CHAPTER 3

Casey

Casey is an 8-year-old second grader at East Valley Elementary. His teacher, Mrs. Bromwell, is having a difficult time with his behavior. Casey has an excessive activity level that makes it difficult for him to attend to one task for longer than 5 or 10 minutes. He seems to have so much energy that he cannot stand still. A typical behavior that causes classroom problems is jumping up and down. Casey will sometimes get up from his desk and starting jumping up and down at what seems to be a frenetic pace. He doesn't stop until Mrs. Bromwell comes over and gently assists him in finding his chair. He has literally worn a hole in the carpet next to his desk from this jumping. Sometimes he will hop around the room, running into other children's desks, knocking over bookcases, and accidentally pushing other children around. He talks "a mile a minute," but he rarely says anything that is of interest to the other children. Casey is in perpetual motion, as if he is being driven to the point of frenzy. Needless to say, this kind of behavior gets on everyone's nerves. He is very unpopular with the other children because he is always accidentally tripping over someone or ruining someone's art project by spilling paint or glue. He even gets in trouble during recess, either because he's moving too fast to listen to the instructions of the game, or because he won't let another student have a turn when he's fixated on a particular activity. For example, he refuses to relinquish the bat until he gets a base hit. Mrs. Bromwell has had many active second graders in her 15 years of teaching, but she has never seen a child like Casey.

Casey's behavior is Mrs. Bromwell's main concern because she feels that it interferes with the work of the whole class. Casey can't stay focused on his work, so he inadvertently bothers the students who are trying to stay on task. Mrs. Bromwell is also concerned about Casey's academics. His handwriting is completely illeg-

ible, and she believes his reading and math skills are well below grade level; however, she's not certain she's getting an accurate evaluation of his abilities because of his attentional difficulties. Mrs. Bromwell thinks that attentional difficulties are preventing others from seeing Casey's strengths, but she doesn't know what to do about it. She wanted to refer him for special education evaluation but was told by her principal that Casey would not qualify because his standardized test scores revealed he was functioning within the average range for his grade placement. Even when Mrs. Bromwell looked up the scores in his cumulative folder, she didn't believe it.

Background Information:

Casey was referred for a special education evaluation in kindergarten. His kindergarten teacher wrote on the referral that she had never seen a child as distracted as Casey. She felt that his problems were so significant that having him repeat kindergarten would do little for him. Casey was given a neurological evaluation as part of the assessment. The neurologist determined that Casey was indeed neurologically impaired and diagnosed attention-deficit disorder with hyperactivity. He prescribed medication to treat his activity level and distractibility problems. For nearly a year following this evaluation, Casey took Ritalin to control his attentional problems. With the help of this medication, Casey had a very successful year in first grade. It appeared that overnight, his handwriting became legible. His reading and math increased to the 50th percentile for first grade. Casey started playing soccer and began making friends. However, over the summer he began having significant side effects from the Ritalin, including insomnia and facial tics. His insomnia was so bad that he was sleeping less than 2 hours per night. Casey developed "amphetamine eyes," the dark circles characteristic of an individual who is abusing amphetamines. His neurologist tried other medications, Dexedrine and Cylert, but the insomnia did not abate and the facial tics worsened. His parents, Mr. and Mrs. Donovan, decided that Casey would not have any more medication regardless of the educational consequences. Mr. and Mrs. Donovan are upset because even when the medication was stopped, Casey's facial tics continued. The neurologist cannot predict whether or not they will ever stop. So now Casey has one more obvious problem added to his other difficulties. His parents are angry and frustrated. They are of the opinion that the school is not doing all that they should to assist Casey in achieving educational goals. They have hinted that if the school had done a better job with Casey during kindergarten, he never would have been on medication and wouldn't be in the predicament he is in now. It is not surprising that when Casey returned to second grade, he demonstrated the same behaviors that his kindergarten teacher had observed.

 Case Study Activities

PART I:
ROLE PLAYING

Break into groups of four and assume one of the following roles: Mr. Donovan, Mrs. Donovan, Mrs. Bromwell, and Ms. Douglas (the Section 504 Building Coordinator, whose responsibility is to develop educational accommodation plans for students with disabilities). Simulate a problem-solving conference to resolve this situation. Because of the circumstances of this case, Casey may not meet the requirements to qualify for special education services; however, he does require an accommodation plan in order to adapt the environment to meet his educational needs. Be sure to address social, physical, and academic needs in this plan. Provide a written summary of the resolution.

Resolution

_____

_____

_____

_____

_____

_____

_____

PART II:
INDIVIDUAL OR GROUP ANALYSIS

Answer the following questions and be prepared to discuss them in class.

1. What is the relationship between learning disabilities and attention-deficit/hyperactivity disorder?

_____

_____

_____

_____

_____

_____

_____

2. What did the principal mean when she said that Casey would not qualify for special education services because of his standardized test scores? What kinds of evaluation criteria are commonly used to identify learning disabilities?

_____

_____

_____

_____

_____

_____

_____

3. Do you agree that Casey's behavior is a higher priority than his academic functioning at this time? Explain your answer.

_____

_____

_____

_____

_____

_____

_____

4. What kind of a behavior management plan might be effective for this student? Give an example of such a plan and identify specific strategies that would be included.

_____

_____

_____

_____

_____

_____

5. Why are children with attentional problems prescribed stimulant medication? How does this medication work? Are side effects such as Casey's common? Are these medications usually considered to be safe for children?

_____

_____

_____

_____

_____

_____

_____

6. How can the school work with this family to help Casey achieve more success?

_____

_____

_____

_____

_____

_____

_____

_____

David

David is a 13-year-old eighth grader at Heights Middle School. He was diagnosed as having a learning disability in the second grade. His primary learning difficulties currently include a fourth-grade reading level, extreme restlessness, and problems paying attention in class. Previously he spent most of the instructional day in a special education classroom. This year, his parents, Mr. and Mrs. Hetzel, have made it clear to the school that they want David to be in the regular classroom throughout the entire day. They feel that the special education program has been too stigmatizing for their son. David has begun showing some symptoms of depression, which they believe are related to his special classroom placement. He has also started to talk about dropping out of school. For almost 3 years now, Mr. and Mrs. Hetzel have been trying to convince David's teachers that regular classroom placement is the most appropriate for his needs, particularly his social needs. David's teachers, however, have felt that the specialized instruction which he receives in special education is preferable to the socialization experiences he may be missing. This year Mr. and Mrs. Hetzel are seriously worried about David's depression, and they have told the school, in no uncertain terms, that there will be no more special classes for their son.

Background Information:

When David was diagnosed as having a learning disability in the second grade, he was also identified as having severe attention-deficit/hyperactivity disorder. This attentional problem, coupled with a significant reading disability, was considered to be a problem of such magnitude that it could only be treated in a self-contained special education setting. At the time of diagnosis, David was placed on medication for the hyperactivity and distractibility, but he experienced significant side effects and was taken off the medication. Another medication trial was attempted at the age of 10, but again the side effects resurfaced. It was determined that David could not safely tolerate any of the medications that typically control activity and attention problems in children. In the special education classroom, David's teachers were able to provide him with a very structured setting and considerable one-to-one instruction, which they know he could not have received in the regular classroom.

Although Mr. and Mrs. Hetzel seem to be frustrated by David's slow progress in reading, his special education teachers see this progress as being significant. David's parents had hoped that all the intensive special education instruction would bring him up to grade level. Instead, they have seen the gap between grade placement and achievement widening every year since he began special education. This is disheartening enough for Mr. and Mrs. Hetzel, but now that David is experiencing emotional problems, they are starting to think that special education has been extremely detrimental to their child. The special education teachers view David's progress differently. They believe that David would be even further behind if he had not been provided with special education. They also believe that the social and emotional problems that David is now experiencing are nothing in comparison to the negative self-concept he would have if he had been left to fail year after year in regular education.

David's special education teachers are opposed to his being completely mainstreamed. They anticipate he will have many more problems in regular education. In a one-to-one or small-group setting, David is able to fulfill work expectations, but in larger group situations where he does not get individual help, he tends to act out and be disruptive. In the past, teachers in classes in which he has been mainstreamed have viewed him as being disrespectful and causing behavior problems by not paying attention. They have suggested that David continue to receive special education services until he can demonstrate successful functioning in the mainstream.

 ## Case Study Activity

INDIVIDUAL CASE ANALYSIS

If David were assigned to your social studies class, describe how you would socially and academically integrate this student. In a two-page response, (a) identify what you consider to be the four most important factors of this case, (b) explain how you would develop a plan for meeting this adolescent's instructional and social needs, (c) delineate specific instructional and behavioral strategies that would be included in your plan, and (d) comment on related issues that may increase David's success in your class.

_____

_____

_____

_____

_____

_____

_____

_____

_____

_____

Jason

Jason is a 10-year-old third grader at Shores Elementary School. Last year he was diagnosed as having a learning disability and attention-deficit/hyperactivity disorder. He is currently reading on a first-grade level. His auditory processing is so weak that he cannot use phonics for decoding purposes. He also has mild language comprehension problems that result in confusion with regard to his ability to follow classroom directions. His reading problems are complicated by his hyperactivity and distractibility. He can remain seated for a maximum of about 10 minutes at a time, and then only if he is in a room that is relatively free of distractions. He frequently gets out of his seat and wanders around the classroom. During this time, he often bothers other students by talking to them or showing them objects from his pocket. Verbal redirection is generally ineffective. The teacher has to come over to Jason, gently touch his shoulder or arm, and remind him that he should be in his seat working.

Jason has few friends. He is large for his age and, since he was retained once, he is considerably larger than his third-grade peers. Jason is considered to be the class clown who is always in trouble. His poor motor coordination causes him to frequently trip and fall. He also has a difficult time participating in playground activities. At recess, he usually wanders around the playground, sometimes spinning himself around until he gets dizzy. The other children consider him to be somewhat odd.

Background Information:

Jason was referred for special education evaluation during the first grade. The referral reasons included both academic and behavioral concerns. Jason's parents, Mr. and Mrs. Ballard, refused permission to evaluate. They asked the school to retain their son in first grade. They felt that since he was immature, another year might give him the added time to develop the academic and behavior skills he was not demonstrating. When Jason showed little progress, Mr. and Mrs. Ballard decided to give permission for the evaluation. Jason's pediatrician took part in the evaluation and strongly recommended that Ritalin be prescribed to help Jason cope with the demands of the classroom. Jason's parents refused to consider this type of treatment. They are adamant in their position that medication not be included in the treatment plan for their son. They have agreed to let Jason receive special education services for 30 minutes per day in the resource room. He is to spend the rest of the instructional day in the regular classroom.

 Case Study Activity

INDIVIDUAL CASE ANALYSIS

As Jason's third-grade teacher, describe how you would academically and socially integrate this child into your classroom. In a two-page response, (a) identify what you consider to be the four most important factors of this case, (b) explain how you would develop a plan for meeting this child's instructional needs, (c) delineate specific instructional and behavioral strategies that would be included in your plan, and (d) comment on related issues that may increase Jason's success in your class.

_____

_____

_____

_____

_____

_____

Jenny

Jenny is a 7-year-old second grader at Lennox Elementary School. She is a very bright child who has been diagnosed with attention-deficit disorder by an independent evaluator outside of school. Her pediatrician recommended that Jenny be medicated with Ritalin to increase her attention in school. Her parents, Mr. and Mrs. Geissler, do not feel that she needs the medication at this point because her grades are good and she seems to be enjoying school. However, Mr. and Mrs. Geissler believe that she could do a little better if she were seated in the front of the room. The psychologist who completed Jenny's evaluation for attention-deficit disorder recommended this accommodation for Jenny. When Mrs. Geissler went to Jenny's teacher, Mr. Leiter, with this request, he reacted unfavorably. In fact, he told Mrs. Geissler that since Jenny was not a special education student, she could not receive any special modifications or services. He also told her that it was his practice to move the students around every 6 weeks, allowing everyone the opportunity to benefit from being in the front of the class. Mrs. Geissler was disappointed, but she didn't want to cause problems so she just let the matter go. However, on the drive home, when she had time to rethink the situation, she became angry. Since Jenny was struggling with this problem and the other children in Mr. Leiter's class weren't, she didn't understand why he couldn't provide this one, simple accommodation for her.

The next day, Mrs. Geissler stopped in to see the principal to ask him to intercede on Jenny's behalf. The principal told her that he was sorry, but he couldn't help her because he needed to support his faculty in their instructional decisions. When she pressed him again, he answered by saying that he wasn't going to get involved in a situation that had already been addressed by one of his most respected teachers, and then he added, "Do you know how hard it is to get male teachers at the elementary school level?" Mrs. Geissler drove home feeling more frustrated than ever.

Background Information:

Mr. Leiter was recently overheard in the faculty lounge telling his colleagues that attention-deficit disorder was "a bunch of baloney," and that this label was just an excuse for "laziness or ignorance." He has been teaching at Lennox for 7 years now and proudly proclaims that he's the only teacher in the building whose classroom isn't used as a "dumping ground" for "those special education types."

 ## Case Study Activity

INDIVIDUAL OR GROUP CASE ANALYSIS

Answer the following questions and be prepared to discuss them in class.

1. Is Mr. Leiter correct in assuming that he does not have to provide accommodations to a student who does not have a special education diagnosis? What laws might influence this case?

_____

_____

_____

_____

_____

_____

_____

2. What do you think of this principal's perspective? What are some strengths and weaknesses of his position?

_____

_____

_____

_____

_____

_____

_____

3. Why didn't Mr. and Mrs. Geissler have Jenny diagnosed with attention-deficit disorder through the special education program at school? Would there be any advantages to an independent evaluation?

_____

_____

_____

_____

_____

_____

_____

4. If Jenny is making satisfactory grades, why does she need the accommodations her parents have requested?

_____

_____

_____

_____

_____

_____

_____

5. If you were one of Mr. Leiter's colleagues, how could you describe attention-deficit disorder to him in a way that might help him better understand and accept this disability?

_____

_____

_____

_____

_____

_____

6. What would you do if you were Jenny's parent? Would you just drop the request and hope for the best for Jenny this year in spite of Mr. Leiter, or would you continue to pursue a modification that you believe is in your child's best interest? Explain your answer.

_____

_____

_____

_____

_____

_____

Joseph

Joseph is a 6-year-old kindergarten student at Silver Maple Elementary School. He has been identified as having attention-deficit/hyperactivity disorder. The problems that this child presents in the classroom are inadequate readiness, hyperactivity, and distractibility. While his classmates can sit in circle for approximately 10 minutes at a time, Joseph can last for only a minute or two at the most. After that time has lapsed, he will invariably start grabbing at the other children, rolling around on the floor, making animal noises, or engaging in other distracting behaviors. In terms of readiness skills, he cannot identify the letters of the alphabet, he has a mild articulation problem, and he displays poor fine motor skills. Socially, he does not interact with his classmates unless one of them has a toy or game that he wants. In that case, he will grab it from the student and run away. If the other student resists, Joseph will use physical aggression to get his way. The kindergarten teacher has 24 children in this class with an aide who assists for 1 hour of the 2½ hour day.

Background Information:

Joseph started kindergarten last fall and was taken out by his parents after 2 weeks of school. His teacher identified excessive activity level, impulsivity, and short attention span as problems that were precluding his successful adjustment to school. The kindergarten teacher and parents were in agreement that Joseph was too immature at that time to begin school. It was felt that given another year, Joseph would be able to have a much more successful kindergarten experience. Now it is 2 weeks into the beginning of the school year and much to the teacher's dismay, Joseph is demonstrating the very same behaviors that he did when he had previously started school.

 Case Study Activity

INDIVIDUAL CASE ANALYSIS

As Joseph's kindergarten teacher, describe how you would socially and academically integrate this child into your classroom. In a two-page response, (a) identify what you consider to be the four most important factors of this case, (b) explain how you would develop a plan for meeting this child's needs, (c) delineate specific instructional and behavior strategies that would be included in your plan, and (d) comment on related issues that may increase Joseph's success in your classroom.

_____

_____

_____

_____

_____

_____

_____

_____

_____

_____

_____

_____

_____

_____

_____

_____

_____

_____

_____

_____

_____

Maria

Maria is a 9-year-old third grader at Oaktrail Elementary School. Her teacher, Mr. Hebert, feels that she is a low average student who does not have the motivation that some of his higher achieving third graders possess. He feels that she could do better than she is currently doing, if she would spend less time daydreaming and more time listening in class. However, she doesn't really cause any problems for him, so he's not especially concerned with her situation.

Maria's father, Mr. Salas, is very concerned about his daughter. He knows she is a bright child who is not achieving as she should be. Maria is receiving Cs and Ds on her report cards. During the past two parent–teacher conferences, Mr. Salas expressed his concern about his daughter's progress to Mr. Hebert who told him that Maria was not applying herself as well as she could be, but "that's the way some kids are." Mr. Salas asked if there were some way that Maria could get some extra help at school. Mr. Hebert told him that they didn't have any special programs for increasing motivation, and he knew Maria would never qualify for special education services because she wasn't failing anything.

Background Information:

Maria is a physically beautiful child with long black hair and huge brown eyes. She has an ingratiating manner that many adults appreciate. When Maria was in preschool, the teacher told her parents that she believed Maria to be gifted in the area of art. Maria did exceptionally well in preschool because most of the curriculum was focused on visual–motor activities and socialization. During kindergarten, Maria was described as a "very capable student" who did well. The kindergarten teacher mentioned that Maria was usually not able to finish her work in the time allotted because of her daydreaming, but this was not a major concern because there was so much variation in kindergarten. In first grade, the teacher referred to Maria as "her wandering princess," saying that Maria had the habit of walking around the room to examine the bulletin board, book table, or contents of the wastepaper basket. This did not really bother the teacher because she felt that Maria was such a sweet child, and she could do the work when she got down to it. The first-grade teacher mentioned that she felt someday Maria would be a famous artist. However, she was concerned enough about Maria's poor listening habits to ask the school nurse to recheck her hearing and make sure that she didn't have a loss that wasn't detected by the last school-wide hearing screen. By the time Maria got to second grade, her grades started dropping, and the teacher started referring to "poor work habits," "weak listening skills," and "daydreaming" problems. Maria started to bring home work to finish at night that her classmates had finished during the day. Still the teacher felt that Maria did not have major problems because "she didn't bother any of the other students."

 Case Study Activity

INDIVIDUAL OR GROUP CASE ANALYSIS

Answer the following questions and be prepared to discuss them in class.

1. Do you see any pattern in the teacher comments regarding Maria's behavior? Should Maria be referred for an attention-deficit disorder evaluation? Why or why not? Is it possible to have attentional problems without hyperactivity?

_____

_____

_____

_____

_____

_____

_____

2. Give four reasons why Maria's previous teachers have not identified a problem with her inattention.

_____

_____

_____

_____

_____

_____

_____

3. Why does Mr. Hebert attribute Maria's problems to motivation? Do you think this type of attribution is common among teachers?

_____

_____

_____

_____

_____

_____

_____

4. If Maria were referred for evaluation, do you think she would qualify for services? What laws might influence Maria's case?

_____

_____

_____

_____

_____

_____

5. What is the prognosis for this child? Would you expect that she would continue to demonstrate the same kind of work? What curriculum factors can you identify that might influence Maria's progress?

_____

_____

_____

_____

_____

_____

_____

6. What kinds of accommodations could Mr. Hebert implement that might increase Maria's classroom performance?

_____

_____

_____

_____

_____

_____

_____

LeShawn

LeShawn is a 15-year-old adolescent at Southeast High School. He has been identified as having attention-deficit/hyperactivity disorder. While he used to have significant difficulty with excessive activity level, causing him to be constantly moving around the room, currently he is struggling with extreme fidgetiness, restlessness, and impulsive behavior.

LeShawn's history class has been particularly difficult this semester. His teacher, Mr. Morton, uses the lecture format for this class. It is his expectation that all of his students conform to the rules. If they do not listen with respect and respond appropriately, he promptly issues a detention slip that requires the student to leave class and go to a special detention room. For every day that a student misses class without an excused absence, Mr. Morton subtracts one point off their final average for the class. Mr. Morton feels that

his discipline plan has been tremendously successful. He is often asked by school officials to give talks about successful discipline practices at the high school level. He explains that the problem with discipline in the schools today is that there is an absence of respect. He feels strongly that it is a sign of disrespect not to listen to the teacher, and that students need to be shown that that kind of behavior will not be tolerated. Mr. Morton believes there can be only one response to that kind of behavior, "The student must be excused from class, and he must pay the consequences of missing the work for that day." The principal, Mrs. Alphonse, backs him up 100 percent. She believes Mr. Morton is one of her best teachers, and she can always trust him to make the best decisions for the students and the school.

The problem in LeShawn's case is that, although he really likes history, he does not have the attention span for 50 minutes of a lecture class. About 10 minutes into class, he will start rocking in his chair, thumping out a beat on his desk, or fidgeting with his notes, book, or pencils. When this happens, Mr. Morton always gives him a warning: If he doesn't stop what he's doing, he'll be sent to detention. That works for about 10 minutes, and then LeShawn will start shuffling his feet or cracking his knuckles. Mr. Morton will then calmly write out the detention slip and walk over to LeShawn's desk, continuing to lecture the whole time. Mr. Morton never raises his voice or gets angry. He believes that the most effective discipline plans are administered in a very calm, firm manner so that the student understands the consequences are not a matter of the teacher losing his temper, but rather of the student not living up to the expectations set for this class.

It's now 5 weeks into the fall semester, and LeShawn has already been issued 15 detention slips by Mr. Morton. He would have been issued more, but Mr. Morton was out with the flu for almost a full week. Although LeShawn is a bright student, it is unlikely that he is going to be able to pass Mr. Morton's class. He has already mentioned dropping out of school to his grandmother, Mrs. Gibbs, who is his guardian. LeShawn feels like there's no point in being in school if he's going to be failing most of his subjects. He feels that he could probably do better if he got a job. Mrs. Gibbs is very concerned, but she doesn't know what to do. She has diabetes which has resulted in the amputation of both legs, and she is also losing her eyesight. It takes all of her energy to take care of LeShawn's laundry and meals. She doesn't have the physical strength to get on a bus and go down to the school to talk to his teachers. She has tried to communicate with the principal, but Mrs. Alphonse told her that she is solidly behind Mr. Morton's discipline plan and that LeShawn needs to learn that off-task behaviors will not be tolerated.

Background Information:

LeShawn was taken away from his parents because of neglect when he was a preschooler. His parents are drug abusers who have been in and out of prison for drug-related convictions. He has lived with his elderly grandmother since the age of 3. LeShawn was referred to a pediatric neurologist for possible lead poisoning by his social worker at the age of 4. At that time, it was determined that he had toxic levels of lead in his body, probably from eating paint chips. He was treated for several years for this toxicity. LeShawn was diagnosed as learning disabled with attention-deficit/hyperactivity disorder in the first grade. Ritalin was prescribed for the activity level problem, and he was placed in a self-contained classroom for the primary years. During the intermediate and middle school years, LeShawn attended resource classes. He continued to take Ritalin with good results. At the end of eighth grade, he was staffed out of special education because his progress had been considerable. He no longer met the requirements for special education services. About this same time, it was discovered that LeShawn was selling his medication instead of using it himself. His social worker, grandmother, and doctor were in agreement—no more Ritalin would be prescribed for LeShawn because of this problem and because of the fact that he was doing so well in school. It was also thought that since LeShawn was an adolescent, he probably would not have as difficult a time with activity level as he had in the past.

Case Study Activities

PART I:
ROLE PLAYING

Break into groups of four or five and assume the roles of LeShawn, Mr. Morton, Mrs. Alphonse, Mr. Smithers (the Section 504 Building Coordinator, whose responsibility is to develop educational accommodation plans for students with disabilities), and Mrs. Gibbs (an optional role). Simulate a problem-solving conference in which these individuals attempt to find a resolution. Provide a written summary of the conference and its resolution.

Resolution

_____

_____

_____

_____

_____

_____

_____

_____

_____

_____

PART II:
INDIVIDUAL OR GROUP CASE ANALYSIS

Answer the following questions and be prepared to discuss them in class.

1. Is there any relationship between LeShawn's past history of toxic lead levels and his attention and learning problems? Explain your answer.

_____

_____

_____

_____

_____

_____

_____

2. Is Mr. Morton an effective teacher? How would you assess his management style?

_____

_____

_____

_____

_____

_____

_____

3. From a legal perspective, does the school have the right to dismiss LeShawn from class on a routine basis for the behavior he is demonstrating? Why or why not?

4. Should LeShawn be put back on his medication to help him be more successful? Is there any way to ensure that he will not resort to selling his medication again?

5. What kinds of accommodations could be used in LeShawn's classes so that he can experience more success at school?

6. What is the prognosis for LeShawn? Do you think that interventions at school can make a difference in this adolescent's life? Explain your answer.

_____

_____

_____

_____

_____

_____

_____

Ramon

Ramon is a 9-year-old student in the third grade at Grand Mesa Elementary School. Last year he was diagnosed as having attention-deficit/hyperactivity disorder. At that time, his pediatrician prescribed Ritalin for him, which has been very beneficial in helping him to sustain attention and curtail activity level in the classroom. Ramon is a very bright youngster who is now making straight As in all subject areas. Everything is going well for him with one exception. At the beginning of the school year, Mr. Rodriguez, his teacher, had a difficult time remembering Ramon's medication, so he finally came up with a solution. His solution involves an alarm clock set according to Ramon's medication schedule—once in the morning and once in the afternoon. When the alarm goes off, Mr. Rodriguez shouts out, "Time for your medicine, Ramon." Ramon then goes down to the office where the school secretary gives him his medicine. This situation causes Ramon a great deal of embarrassment. The other children in the class tease him, and he gets very upset. Yesterday one of the children yelled out, "Ramon, better go get your pill before you go crazy." The whole class, with the exception of Ramon, thought that this was uproariously funny.

Ramon's mother, Mrs. Archuletta, has called Mr. Rodriguez and asked him to find another way to remind himself about Ramon's medicine. He basically told her that she was lucky that he took the time and effort to use the alarm clock technique. Mr. Rodriguez also told her that her son had better get a "thicker skin" because things are not going to get easier "for a kid with all of his problems." He further

informed Mrs. Archuletta that he didn't have to give Ramon his medication and that he was just doing it as a favor. He ended the conversation by saying that if she had any more complaints, she should direct them to the principal. This really hurt Mrs. Archuletta's feelings. She doesn't want to create a major problem, but she also doesn't want her son to continue to endure the teasing associated with his medication. She wonders what the principal's reaction would be.

Background Information:

Ramon had a very difficult time during the primary school years. His problems with activity level and attention made it very difficult for him to do his work or follow teacher directives. By the time he entered second grade, he had developed a very negative image of himself. He told his mother that he was stupid and that his teacher and peers hated him. During his second-grade year, it was a continual battle to get him to go to school each morning. Ramon complained of stomachaches, headaches, leg pains, and backaches so often that Mrs. Archuletta asked his pediatrician to run a series of diagnostic tests to determine the basis of these complaints. Ramon's pediatrician concluded that his problems were probably psychological and referred him for an evaluation, at which point his attention-deficit/hyperactivity disorder was diagnosed. The medication and counseling that Ramon received appeared to go a long way in changing his negative perception of himself.

 **Case Study Activity**

INDIVIDUAL OR GROUP CASE ANALYSIS

Answer the following questions and be prepared to discuss them in class.

1. If you were Ramon's parent, what would you do about this situation?

_____

_____

_____

_____

_____

_____

2. Why do you think Mr. Rodriguez has taken this attitude about Ramon's medication schedule? Does he have the right to refuse to send Ramon to the office to get his medication? Explain your answer.

_____

_____

_____

_____

_____

_____

3. Is Ramon being overly sensitive about what Mr. Rodriguez is doing? Explain your answer.

_____

_____

_____

_____

_____

_____

4. How do you think the principal would respond if Mrs. Archuletta went to him with her concern? What about the superintendent?

_____

_____

_____

_____

_____

_____

_____

5. Can you think of another way that Mr. Rodriguez could remind himself of Ramon's medication schedule?

_____

_____

_____

_____

_____

_____

_____

Affective Needs

CHAPTER 4

Jody

Jody is a 9-year-old third-grade student at Gatesville Elementary School. Her teacher, Ms. Kioness, is quite concerned about her academic and social skills. Jody is a nonreader who appears to have very limited language skills. Although she can compute basic math facts, she has major deficits in reasoning and application of math skills. Ms. Kioness is even more concerned about social integration problems. Jody never smiles or talks to any of the other children, even when they ask her questions. Occasionally, she may shake or nod her head in response, but she rarely speaks. Jody cries frequently for no apparent reason. Ms. Kioness has the impression that the child is afraid to leave her side. Her desk is right next to the teacher's, and she remains there throughout the day. Ms. Kioness has to force her to go out to recess where she stands next to the wall for the entire time. Jody also has a problem with enuresis; she wets herself almost every day. Ms. Kioness has never had a student such as this, and she is really at a loss about what to do for this child.

Background Information:

Jody was kidnapped by her father when she was 2 years old after a bitter divorce and custody battle. The father took both Jody and her 3-year-old brother from their mother, who had custody of the two children. For the past 7 years, Jody and her brother have had little contact with anyone but their father. For most of that time, the family was on the run to avoid the authorities. The father taught the children not to speak to anyone for fear that they would be taken away. He also told them that their mother had repeatedly abused them and would probably kill them if they were returned to her care. During this 7-year period, the children lived with their father in the car or in inexpensive motels. They basically roamed the country, staying mainly in rural areas to avoid detection. The children were discovered by the state police one chilly fall morning. The father had left them alone in the car for an evening of drinking. As he was making his way back to the car late at night, he apparently stumbled and fell into a ravine. After striking his head, he died of a cerebral hemorrhage. It was determined that the children were probably alone in the car for at least a day and a half before they were found by the police.

Although the mother had never given up hope that the children would one day be returned, she expressed uncertainty about integrating them into her new family once Jody and her brother were found. She had remarried 6 years ago, and she now has two other children with her second husband. Her husband has told the authorities that he believes the children would be better off with an adoptive family since they have been gone so long and are so fearful of their mother. Jody's mother has indicated to the teacher that she doesn't know what to do with the children. She describes Jody's behavior at home as being similar to what Ms. Kioness is observing at school, except at home Jody never leaves her brother's side and seems fearful of her mother and stepfather. It's been 2 months now since the children have been returned, and Jody's mother is beginning to wonder if her husband might be right about adoption. She loves her children, but she sometimes feels that her presence is causing their unhappiness. Things don't seem to be getting any better.

Case Study Activity

INDIVIDUAL OR GROUP CASE ANALYSIS

Answer the following questions and be prepared to discuss them in class.

1. Should Ms. Kioness refer Jody for a special education evaluation? Why or why not?

_____

_____

_____

_____

_____

_____

_____

2. Should Ms. Kioness be more concerned with Jody's socialization at this point or with her academic problems? Explain your response.

_____

_____

_____

_____

_____

_____

_____

3. What kinds of strategies could Ms. Kioness use to encourage Jody to talk more?

_____

_____

_____

_____

_____

_____

_____

4. What kinds of strategies could Ms. Kioness use to encourage socialization opportunities for Jody?

_____

_____

_____

_____

_____

_____

_____

5. If you were Ms. Kioness, would you attempt to provide assistance to this family? Why or why not? If you do think that you might be able to help, what types of resources might you use?

_____

_____

_____

_____

_____

_____

_____

6. What should Ms. Kioness do about Jody's enuresis?

_____

_____

_____

_____

_____

_____

_____

7. How could Ms. Kioness help Jody to feel less fearful when she's at school?

_____

_____

_____

_____

_____

_____

_____

8. Do you think that there is a relationship between Jody's language and academic problems and the lifestyle she has led with her father? Explain your response.

_____

_____

_____

_____

_____

_____

_____

_____

_____

Joel

Joel is a 17-year-old adolescent at Kensington High School. He is a popular student at this private school where he has been very active in athletics as well as social clubs. Last year he was president of his class. This year things are very different for this student. He has started missing quite a bit of school and has recently dropped the swim team and the chess club, two of his favorite extracurricular activities. In previous years, Joel was always at the center of a crowd of students, laughing and joking. This year he frequently seems to be by himself. It is the first year he has not had a steady girlfriend. His grades have dropped from a 3.5 average to a 2.2.

Joel's math teacher, Mr. Dubois, who is also the advisor of the chess club, is disgusted with Joel's behavior. He has told other faculty members that Joel has probably gotten into the drug scene. Mr. Shaw, his history teacher and former swim team coach, thinks that Joel has just become lazy. He feels that a lot of kids from wealthy families such as Joel's have things too easy, so there's no motivation to keep striving for goals. Ms. Jardin, Joel's English teacher, does not agree

with the other teachers. She has become increasingly disturbed by Joel's steady decline. She has noticed that while his manner of dress used to be impeccable, it now appears that he is wearing the same clothes over and over. As of late, it has occurred to Ms. Jardin that Joel is not bathing or observing other basic hygiene practices. When Ms. Jardin has carefully approached him about how things are going or how he's feeling, Joel has responded by telling her that he's tired because he's been studying too hard and staying up too late at night. Ms. Jardin knows this can hardly be true because the quality of his work has dropped dramatically.

Last week an incident occurred that has caused Ms. Jardin to have additional concern about Joel. A national news report about an adolescent suicide pact received quite a bit of media attention. During this same week Joel wrote a theme on alienation and mentioned suicide as an alternative to "the day-to-day struggle to search for meaning in life." The mention of suicide in combination with Joel's behavior was enough to alarm Ms. Jardin. She called Joel's parents, Mr. and Mrs. Richert, to request a conference. Mr. Richert was on a business trip in Hong Kong, and Mrs. Richert was on a ski trip in Aspen. Ms. Jardin asked the housekeeper to have Mrs. Richert call her at her home number as soon as possible. Three days later Mrs. Richert called Ms. Jardin at 11:30 P.M. When Ms. Jardin explained her concern for Joel and his mention of suicide, Mrs. Richert seemed to become irritated. She remarked that it was normal for teenagers to be depressed and that she herself had been depressed for all 4 years of high school. Mrs. Richert also mentioned that she was upset over Joel's latest report card, stating that if his teachers spent as much time worrying about his academics as they did worrying about his feelings, his grades might be a whole lot better. She then abruptly hung up.

Background Information:

Joel has always done extremely well in school, both academically and socially. He has never shown any symptoms of depression prior to this year. Joel is the only child of wealthy parents, who are very much involved in the community. Because his parents have such busy lives, he is alone with the housekeeper much of the time. Mr. and Mrs. Richert are proud of their son and his achievements. Mrs. Richert can't help but notice that Joel is behaving differently, but she doesn't want to make a "big deal" about it. She is afraid that talking about depression will only make it worse. Her father committed suicide while he was being treated for depression. Mr. Richert, because of his busy schedule and traveling, is not really aware of any change in Joel.

 ## Case Study Activities

PART I:
ROLE PLAYING

Break into groups of four and assume the following roles: Mrs. Richert, Ms. Jardin, Mr. Dubois, and Mr. Shaw. Simulate a problem-solving conference in which the participants attempt to address Joel's emotional and academic problems. Following the role-playing activity, write a summary of the resolution.

Resolution

_____

_____

_____

_____

_____

_____

_____

_____

_____

_____

_____

PART II:
INDIVIDUAL OR GROUP CASE ANALYSIS

Answer the following questions and be prepared to discuss them in class.

1. What should Ms. Jardin do about this problem? Has she fulfilled her responsibilities by informing the parents of her concerns, or does she need to do more?

_____

_____

_____

_____

_____

_____

_____

_____

2. Based on the information in this case study, do you think that Joel's depression is severe or mild? Is there specific information in this case that leads you to this conclusion? Explain your response.

_____

_____

_____

_____

_____

_____

_____

3. Do you think that encouraging adolescents to talk about their feelings regarding suicide increases the likelihood that they will attempt suicide? Why or why not?

_____

_____

_____

_____

_____

_____

_____

4. Why do you think that Joel's mother has responded in such a negative way to Ms. Jardin's concerns? What kinds of events in her background may have influenced her response?

_____

_____

_____

_____

_____

_____

_____

5. Other than identifying potential cases of suicide in their students and informing the parents, is there anything else that secondary education teachers can do to help students who are dealing with significant bouts of depression?

_____

_____

_____

_____

_____

_____

_____

6. Do you think that Joel should be referred to a residential facility for treatment? Why or why not?

_____

_____

_____

_____

_____

_____

_____

Levonda

Levonda is a 6-year-old first grader at Willowbrook Elementary School. She spent her kindergarten school year in a noncategorical preschool program for special needs children. Levonda's diagnosis of emotional disturbance was based on her extreme withdrawal resulting from a pattern of sexual abuse, which this child endured for an extended period of time. Levonda also developed a phobia to school which makes it very difficult for her to separate from her mother, Mrs. Rand. Although Levonda is still considered to be a very disturbed child, her special education teacher, Mrs. Holmes, feels that her needs could be met in the regular classroom environment since she does not have academic problems. Mrs. Holmes has so many autistic children in her classroom that she feels Levonda won't be provided with the type of role models that would help her to learn appropriate social skills. She strongly recommended that Levonda be placed into a regular first-grade classroom.

Levonda's first-grade teacher, Ms. Chinn, is an energetic young woman in her first year of teaching. When her principal told her that Levonda would be included in her class, Ms. Chinn was not upset. As a matter of fact, she felt complimented that the principal, Mrs. Shapiro, would give her such a challenging child to work with during her first year in the classroom. Ms. Chinn took it as a vote of confidence from her administrator. She looked forward to meeting Levonda and helping her work through some of her problems.

On the first day of school, Ms. Chinn met Levonda and Mrs. Rand at the front door. In her softest and most reassuring voice, Ms. Chinn told her how happy she was that Levonda would be one of her students, and then she gently picked up Levonda's hand to walk her to her desk. As soon as she touched Levonda's hand, Levonda began to scream in a loud, high-pitched voice. Ms. Chinn immediately dropped her hand and Levonda ran to her mother, continuing to scream for the next 5 minutes. Ms. Chinn was very upset, but she tried to compose herself to greet the other students. When Levonda finally stopped screaming, her mother firmly told her that it was time for her to leave, but that she would be back after school. Levonda started to scream again, so Mrs. Rand asked Ms. Chinn to hold her until she left the building. As Ms. Chinn restrained Levonda, she began to cry and scream louder. She also started kicking Ms. Chinn. At this point some of the other first graders began to cry. The principal walked by the classroom and came in with a very concerned look on her face and said, "Ms. Chinn, please get your class under control!"

After about 10 minutes, Levonda's screams were reduced to sobs and quiet whimpering. She found her way to a corner and stayed there for the next hour. Ms. Chinn decided to leave her alone a while, hoping that she would slowly adjust to the classroom in her own way. However, Ms. Chinn could not ignore the fact that Levonda had picked up a rag doll in the book corner and had begun masturbating with it. Since Levonda had pulled her dress up and was thrusting the rag doll in such a fashion as to attract attention, many of her classmates had noticed the commotion in the book corner. Ms. Chinn got up from her desk and took the doll from Levonda and pulled down her dress. Levonda began screaming again. It took her 15 minutes to settle down this time.

Ms. Chinn is seriously considering resignation. The only peace she has in her first-grade classroom is when Levonda is with Mrs. Holmes for an hour and 15 minutes in the afternoon. Levonda's special education teacher is sympathetic about the first-grade classroom situation, but she really feels that Levonda just needs more time with typical peers. "It will get better for you and Levonda," Mrs. Holmes says. Ms. Chinn has no reason to believe this is true. In the 4 weeks that Levonda has been with Ms. Chinn, her pattern of behavior remains the same on a daily basis. Every morning she cries loudly and has to be restrained when her mother leaves. She stays in the corner and refuses to be part of the class, screaming when Ms. Chinn or her classmates try to approach her. Ms. Chinn cannot get her interested in any of the first-grade activities, and Levonda seems intent on spending much of her time masturbating in the book corner or at her desk. The principal recently told Ms. Chinn that she has had a number of complaints from parents, and she suggested that some significant changes be made so that this first-grade classroom is a more comfortable place for all the children. Ms. Chinn has no idea how to accomplish this.

Background Information:

When Levonda started preschool at the age of 3, Mrs. Rand would drop her off on her way to work. Mr. Rand would then pick her up from preschool, as he was unemployed. He was in charge of Levonda's afternoon care. It was during this time period that Levonda began having significant behavior problems. A routine visit to the pediatrician revealed that Levonda had been sexually abused. A social worker was called in to help the family. Levonda's father left the home and entered a counseling program. He came back into the home after he had successfully completed the program. A year later, another routine visit to the pediatrician revealed that once again Levonda was being sexually abused. This time Mrs. Rand divorced Mr. Rand, but Levonda's behavior had deteriorated to the point that the social worker referred her to Child Find. She was diagnosed as seriously emotionally disturbed with extreme withdrawal, separation anxiety, tactile defensiveness, and depressive symptoms. Full-time, special education programming was recommended for her kindergarten school year.

 ## Case Study Activities

PART I:
ROLE PLAYING

Break into groups of four and simulate an IEP meeting in which Levonda's educational needs are addressed. Use the IEP form included on page 96 to write these goals. The following roles should be assumed by group members: Mrs. Rand, Ms. Chinn, Mrs. Shapiro, and Mrs. Holmes. During this meeting, the group should: (a) review current functioning, (b) identify strengths and weaknesses, (c) develop short and long term goals, (d) describe possible teaching strategies that will be used to achieve these goals, (e) explain the services to be provided, and (f) determine responsibility with regard to carrying out the educational plan.

PART II:
INDIVIDUAL OR GROUP CASE ANALYSIS

Answer the following questions and be prepared to discuss them in class.

1. Why is Levonda having such a difficult time separating from her mother? What strategies should Ms. Chinn try to help her with this separation?

_____

_____

_____

_____

_____

_____

_____

2. Is Ms. Chinn getting the support she needs from her principal? Is it the principal's responsibility to assist the teachers with management problems such as these?

_____

_____

_____

_____

_____

_____

_____

3. What should Ms. Chinn do about Levonda's masturbation?

_____

_____

_____

_____

_____

_____

_____

4. Should Levonda be in a regular first-grade classroom such as Ms. Chinn's? Why or why not?

_____

_____

_____

_____

_____

_____

5. What should Ms. Chinn do about the parent complaints?

_____

_____

_____

_____

_____

_____

6. What resources might Ms. Chinn use to help her with Levonda?

_____

_____

_____

_____

_____

_____

_____

7. What strategies can Ms. Chinn use to encourage Levonda to socialize with her peers? How can she address the problem of tactile defensiveness with this child?

_____

_____

_____

_____

_____

_____

_____

_____

Lionel

Lionel is a 14-year-old sixth grader at Welby Heights Middle School. Last year the pupil assessment team identified Lionel as having an emotional disturbance and staffed him into a full-time special education class. The evaluation report described him as an "extremely defiant adolescent who frequently uses verbal and physical aggression to get his way." Lionel is well-known by all of the teachers in the building as a student who is quick to anger and often resorts to violence. Last year Lionel slapped his English teacher in the face and stomped on her glasses until they were crushed. He also slashed the tires of the physical education teacher while the teacher was watching from a window. Lionel knew the teacher was watching, and continued the act defiantly. He is usually involved in several altercations each week. When he is not in trouble, it is because he wasn't in school for the day.

Absenteeism is also a big problem. The district truancy officer knows Lionel well.

Mr. Andreason, the principal, expelled Lionel for half of the school year last year for attacking another one of his teachers. The year before, Mr. Andreason suspended Lionel for 45 days of the school year. These suspensions, expulsions, and Lionel's absenteeism have resulted in a 3-year stint in the sixth grade. Mr. Andreason has laughingly told Lionel that if he doesn't change his behavior, he's going to be driving to the sixth grade pretty soon. Mr. Andreason has secretly wished that the truancy officer weren't so conscientious about picking up Lionel when he's out of school. Welby Heights runs a whole lot smoother without Lionel. Mr. Andreason worked to get Lionel placed in special education, and he was hopeful that this placement would help control Lionel's aggressive behavior.

School District #1
Individualized Educational Program

Student: _____

Current Functioning	Long-Term Goals	Short-Term Objectives

He was shocked to discover yesterday that not only was this placement not reducing Lionel's aggressive incidents, but it was also preventing him from "keeping my school safe."

Yesterday Lionel got in a fight with a fellow student whom he had been teasing. Lionel struck the boy so hard that he had to have 15 stitches above his lip. He also tore the boy's shirt off his chest. Mr. Andreason felt that this attack was especially hateful because his victim was a student with Down syndrome who couldn't really fight back. When Mr. Andreason told the special education teacher, Mr. Dawson, that he was going to suspend Lionel for a month, he was surprised when Mr. Dawson told him that he probably could not legally take that action since Lionel was now identified as a student with an emotional disability. Mr. Andreason can't believe that there's a law that is going to force him to keep a violent student in school when other students might come to harm.

Background Information:

Lionel lives with his mother and six other siblings in a motel room in one of the roughest neighborhoods in the city. They live from hand to mouth and move around often. Social services has been called in on several occasions to evaluate the family living situation, but it is hard for them to track the family down and follow up on reports of neglect. Lionel has been referred for special education evaluation every year since the first grade. His school history has been characterized by fighting, stealing, lying, and threatening peers and teachers. Every year the forms for evaluation were sent home with Lionel, but they were never returned. His mother, Mrs. Miller, did not sign the paperwork for the

evaluation until this year, when Mr. Andreason decided to pursue this situation. He and the school social worker found Lionel's mother in one of the motels in the area. Although it was 1:00 in the afternoon, the mother was in bed, surrounded by several small children who were watching television. Mrs. Miller did not get out of bed, but she sat up and gave her visitors her attention, asking the children to turn the television down. When the social worker asked her if she were ill, she replied that she was just tired. Mr. Andreason explained some of the difficulties that Lionel was having at school. She was apparently aware of these problems, but she told the principal and social worker that she could not control Lionel's behavior and that she rarely sees him. Sometimes he doesn't even come home at night. Several times the family has had to move without knowing where Lionel was, but he eventually caught up with them. Mr. Andreason explained the testing to her and obtained her permission for evaluation. He came back a month later to get her signature on the placement papers. On this visit, he could not help but notice that Mrs. Miller was pregnant.

Having observed the family's living conditions, the principal and the social worker were disturbed. They discussed the lack of supervision in reference to Lionel's problems. Mr. Andreason felt that it was necessary to follow through with this evaluation for Lionel's sake and for the sake of everyone else at Welby Heights. He has a lot of respect for the way Mr. Dawson works with troubled students, and he was hopeful that the special education teacher could help Lionel. He did not anticipate that special education placement would now serve to protect Lionel from certain disciplinary actions.

 ## Case Study Activity

INDIVIDUAL OR GROUP CASE ANALYSIS

Answer the following questions and be prepared to discuss them in class.

1. Why do you think that a previous administrator didn't get permission for testing so that Lionel could have received help in the elementary school years?

_____

_____

_____

_____

_____

_____

_____

2. Do you think that keeping Lionel in the sixth grade for 3 years was an appropriate measure for the school to take? Why or why not?

_____

_____

_____

_____

_____

_____

_____

3. Do you think that it is possible for Lionel's behavior to change? What kind of strategies would you recommend for a student such as this? Give three examples.

_____

_____

_____

_____

_____

_____

_____

4. Is there anything that the school can do to assist Lionel's family? Explain your response. What kind of impact does this lifestyle have on growth and development?

_____

_____

_____

_____

5. What is Mr. Dawson referring to when he told Mr. Andreason that Lionel probably could not be suspended or expelled now that he had been staffed into the special education program? What laws protect this student's right to an education?

6. What legal options does a school have in terms of dealing with violence in this type of situation?

7. What is the prognosis for Lionel? Do you think there are other children and adolescents in this country in similar situations? How extensive do you feel this problem is?

Miguel

Miguel is a 10-year-old fifth grader at Meadowview Elementary. He was diagnosed as emotionally disturbed when he was in third grade. At that time he was placed in a self-contained classroom where he stayed for 2 years. This year Miguel has been assigned to Mr. Rivera's fifth-grade class because of the school district's move toward more inclusive environments for students with disabilities. It has been 2 weeks since the beginning of the school year, and Mr. Rivera is perplexed about the situation in his classroom. Initially, he was not opposed to having Miguel in his classroom, even though other teachers made comments and rolled their eyes whenever the principal referred to the placement change for Miguel. Mr. Rivera views himself as a "take charge" kind of teacher who enjoys the challenges that his students present to him. Now he's having second thoughts about Miguel's place in his classroom.

Miguel has many positive qualities that Mr. Rivera tries to focus on and reinforce. He's a kind child who has a gentle, sensitive nature and a good sense of humor (when he's feeling well). However, Miguel also has many troublesome behaviors that seem to get more attention than his positive behaviors. One example of these behaviors is Miguel's persistence in turning statements around to negate whatever is being said. For example, when Sara's mother came to pick her up for a dentist's appointment one day, Miguel saw her at the door and immediately began calling out, "Sara, that is *not* your mother. I know for a fact that woman is *not* your mother." He does the same thing in class with whatever facts Mr. Rivera is trying to teach, such as states and their capitals. All of a sudden, he'll start calling out, "Springfield is *not* the capital of Illinois!" When Mr. Rivera tries to reason with him, Miguel tearfully defends his actions by saying, "Mr. Rivera, I really like you, but I cannot let you lie to all these students." And he will persist even when shown a map of the states with the capitals written on it. "The people who made this map are lying!" he will insist. Mr. Rivera tries to ignore this behavior, but it is difficult to do because it is so disruptive.

The most troublesome aspect of having Miguel in the classroom is his persistent self-abusive behavior. Miguel frequently uses pens, pencils, rulers, or other objects to cut the inside of his forearms. This happens several times a day, usually when Mr. Rivera is helping another student. Miguel will begin by running the pen or pencil lightly up and down his arm, and then he will gradually increase the pressure until he begins bleeding. When he is engaging in this injurious behavior, he gets a glazed expression on his face. Sometimes Mr. Rivera doesn't even know it's happening until one of his students tells him that, "Miguel is at it again." He will then run over and take the object away. Usually after cutting himself, Miguel seems to be more relaxed. It is almost like the injury provides him with some kind of psychological relief. Miguel often has to be taken to the nurse's office for first aid. Once he had to be taken to the hospital because he had cut into an artery. This behavior is frustrating for Mr. Rivera because he feels like he has to watch Miguel every minute, or he'll hurt himself. He thinks that his other 25 students are being neglected because he has to give so much attention to Miguel. Mr. Rivera is also starting to lose some confidence in his ability to handle his classroom, which really depresses him. He has always enjoyed teaching, but this year he's starting to dread many days.

Background Information:

Miguel was 8 years old when he witnessed his father shoot his pregnant mother and baby sister to death in an incident of domestic violence. Since the shooting, he has suffered severe emotional distress that has been manifested in self-injurious behavior and mutism. For 1 full year after his mother's death, Miguel did not utter a word. He and his three surviving brothers were put into separate foster homes. It was later uncovered that Miguel's first foster father sexually abused him repeatedly. No one knew at the time because he was not speaking. Miguel was in that abusive home for a year when the foster family abruptly left town without any explanation to the authorities. Miguel was left alone in the rented house with another foster child for 2 days before the landlord discovered that the family had abandoned them. Miguel was transferred to another foster care family where he stayed for 6 months. It was during this time that he began to talk and physically abuse himself. The foster family asked that Miguel be removed because they could not deal with the self-injurious behavior. Miguel now lives in a group home.

Case Study Activity

INDIVIDUAL OR GROUP CASE ANALYSIS

Answer the following questions and be prepared to discuss them in class.

1. Should Miguel be placed in a self-contained special education classroom? Why or why not?

2. What should Mr. Rivera do about Miguel's self-injurious behavior? Explain four specific strategies that you would use to decrease this behavior if you were his teacher.

3. What strategies should Mr. Rivera use to decrease Miguel's odd behavior of negating facts?

4. Do you think the other students in Mr. Rivera's class are suffering because of the inclusion of Miguel? Explain your response.

_____

_____

_____

_____

_____

_____

5. What is the prognosis for Miguel? Can you think of any factors that could enhance this prognosis?

_____

_____

_____

_____

_____

_____

_____

6. What kinds of strategies can Mr. Rivera use to relieve his stress and start to get his confidence back?

_____

_____

_____

_____

_____

_____

7. Why do you think that Miguel injures himself? Why do you think that Miguel is fixated on disputing facts in his classroom?

_____

_____

_____

_____

_____

_____

_____

_____

_____

Mitchell

Mitchell is an 11-year-old fourth grader at Alameda Elementary School. He was identified as having a serious emotional disturbance at the age of 7. Since that time he has been in a self-contained classroom for students with behavioral disorders.

This morning, when he was standing in line waiting to enter the school building, he was involved in an altercation with a second-grade child. During the fight, Mitchell pulled a plastic knife out of his back pocket and began stabbing the other boy. Since the knife was a toy, the second grader was not hurt, but the effect of the incident was horrifying to the children who were observing the fight and to the teachers who broke it up. The principal, Mr. Reid, called Mitchell's mother, Mrs. Fazano, and told her to come and get her child immediately, as he was expelled for the remainder of the school year. The school district has a policy of expelling all students who bring weapons or facsimiles of weapons to school.

Mrs. Fazano is outraged that her son is being expelled. She has had numerous disagreements with Mr. Reid in the past as a result of the way he has disciplined Mitchell. She feels than her son receives punishment that is much more severe than what the other children receive for the same infractions. Mrs. Fazano is also upset because she has no childcare for Mitchell, and she cannot afford to pay anyone to supervise him. She has just been hired at a new job which she feels is really going to work out for her, but she knows she will not be able to keep it if Mitchell is not in school. Mrs. Fazano is going to call the Legal Aid Advocacy Center for Children with Disabilities and try to get some help.

Background Information:

When Mitchell was initially identified as having an emotional disturbance, the pupil assessment evaluation report described him as a "deeply troubled child who has demonstrated a marked pattern of physical and verbal aggression over an extended period of time." The report recommended that Mitchell's behavior required a self-contained setting in which he could be provided the necessary support for his disability, support which he needed to develop anger control strategies. Unfortunately, the special education classroom has not been able to provide Mitchell with the assistance that was recommended. Since he started in this program in the second grade, he has had 12 different teachers. Most of these teachers were not certified in the area in which they were teaching. They were hired as substitutes or temporary teachers until a fully certified special education teacher could be found. Alameda Elementary is in a low socioeconomic area of the city that has major problems with crime. It is difficult to attract any teachers, much less those who are interested and trained in the area of emotional disturbance. Alameda's program for students with emotional disturbance serves students who have some of the most serious problems in the whole school district, and many of these problems are manifested in aggressive behavior.

Mr. Reid is very familiar with Mitchell because he is frequently sent down to his office for incidents related to uncontrollable behavior. The principal knows that many of Mitchell's school problems are due to inadequacies in his special education program. He wishes he could find a good special education teacher for that classroom. He knows it would make his job a lot easier. He also feels that Mitchell's mother is partly to blame because she doesn't seem to have any control over his behavior at home or at school. Mr. Reid has been the principal at Alameda for more years than he'd like to count, and he's starting to feel worn down by the problems of the community. He'd like to see parents take responsibility for their children's problems instead of leaving everything to the schools. He's glad that he can call Mrs. Lu, the school district's Discipline Officer, in case Mrs. Fazano creates a commotion about this expulsion. Mrs. Lu really knows how to play "hard ball" with the parents of hard-to-handle kids.

 ## Case Study Activities

PART I:
ROLE PLAYING

Break into groups of four with each student assuming one of the following roles: Mr. Reid, Mrs. Fazano, Mr. Montoya (an attorney for the Legal Aid Advocacy Center for Children with Disabilities), and Mrs. Lu. Simulate a problem-solving conference in which these individuals attempt to reach a resolution for this case. Write a summary of the results of this meeting.

Resolution

_____

_____

_____

_____

_____

_____

_____

PART II:
INDIVIDUAL OR GROUP CASE ANALYSIS

Answer the following questions and be prepared to discuss them in class.

1. Does the school have the legal right to expel this child? Why or why not? What laws might influence this case?

_____

_____

_____

_____

_____

_____

2. What do you think should be done for Mitchell? Should he be allowed to stay at this school, should he be expelled, or should he be transferred to another school? Explain your answer.

_____

_____

_____

_____

_____

_____

_____

_____

3. Has Mitchell received an appropriate education at Alameda Elementary? Explain your answer.

_____

_____

_____

_____

_____

_____

_____

_____

4. In your opinion, what can be done to attract teachers to assume challenging positions at schools such as Alameda?

_____

_____

_____

_____

_____

_____

_____

_____

5. If you were Mitchell's teacher, how would you work with Mrs. Fazano to establish a home–school behavior management plan? What would be some of the essential features of this plan? Identify some of the possible constraints you would have in working with this parent, and describe how you would overcome these.

_____

_____

_____

_____

_____

_____

_____

6. What is the prognosis for this child? Do you think school intervention can make a difference for Mitchell? Why or why not?

_____

_____

_____

_____

_____

_____

_____

Rinna

Rinna is a 5-year-old who started kindergarten at Crawford Elementary School 2 weeks ago. She has been diagnosed as emotionally disturbed. This child has never had any preschool experience nor any interaction with other children. In addition to emotional problems, Rinna has delayed language and readiness skills. She confuses colors and cannot consistently identify shapes. She does not know the alphabet or number concepts past 3. Rinna has a difficult time holding crayons and pencils for writing purposes. Over the years, Mrs. Vasquez, the kindergarten teacher, has had experience teaching many students who are not prepared to meet school expectations, but Rinna's problems are far more troubling because of her behavioral difficulties.

Whenever Rinna becomes the least bit frustrated or tired, she pretends that she is a dog. She gets down on her hands and knees and begins barking in an animated fashion. Rinna also licks the floor, furniture, and any children in her immediate vicinity. Most of the kindergarten students think that this behavior is uproariously funny, except for the ones who are being licked, many of whom end up in tears. Rinna will not respond to redirection or to Mrs. Vasquez's requests to stop the behavior. The only way that Mrs. Vasquez has been able to stop the behavior is by literally chasing Rinna around the room until she catches her. Eventually Rinna end ups in tears when Mrs. Vasquez finally gets her to stop. She will often continue to cry loudly for about 10 minutes, usually screaming, "You hate me—I hate you too—I hate all of you." Obviously this has an unsettling impact on the rest of the kindergartners. Since Rinna has limited readiness skills, she is frustrated for most of the time she is working on kindergarten curriculum. The only part of the morning that does not seem upsetting for her is the time she spends with Mr. Asante, the special education teacher who comes into Mrs. Vasquez's class for 30 minutes each day. During this time, Rinna seldom exhibits any of the bizarre behavior that characterizes the remainder of the kindergarten morning.

Mrs. Vasquez is a 15-year veteran kindergarten teacher who is feeling completely overwhelmed by this 5-year-old. Last week two angry parents called the principal with complaints regarding Rinna's licking behavior. The principal told Mrs. Vasquez that she had better "get the situation under control immediately." Mrs. Vasquez is well aware of the problems in her classroom. She knows that her kindergarten students are not learning what they need to be learning because of the distraction of Rinna's behavior. She is very much concerned that her kindergartners are 3 weeks behind in their curriculum. This year it is taking much longer to accomplish instructional objectives because of the time she spends controlling Rinna's behavior. Keeping on schedule with school district curriculum objectives has always been a priority with Mrs. Vasquez. It bothers her that she does not feel as if she is in control of the situation. She's wondering if she should switch to third grade next year.

Background Information:

From birth to age 2½, Rinna was cared for mainly by her maternal grandmother who lived with the family. This childcare situation was necessitated by the fact that Rinna's mother, Mrs. Bessant, was a very disturbed woman who suffered from manic-depressive illness. Rinna was well cared for by her grandmother until the woman died suddenly of a stroke. From that time on, she was cared for by her mother, but Mrs. Bessant was so ill that she simply could not meet her child's daily needs. Every day she put Rinna out in a fenced yard

with two family dogs. Rinna would stay in the yard all day long, eating and drinking out of the dog dishes until her father would return from the fields. He would bring her in, clean her up, and put her to bed. Since he was a farmer, he was in the fields from sunup to sunset on most days. On occasions, when he came in early because of rain, he would find Rinna in the doghouse. When he questioned his wife about it, she would tell him that she tried to get Rinna to come in the house but the child would not leave the company of her pets. Mr. Bessant knew that the childcare situation was not satisfactory, but he did not know the extent of the neglect. His growing uneasiness coupled with Rinna's slow development prompted him to ask his mother to come and live with them so that she could assist in the care of both his wife and daughter. Just before she arrived, Mrs. Bessant committed suicide.

When the paternal grandmother moved in, she knew immediately that something was drastically wrong with her grandchild. She convinced her son to take Rinna to the pediatrician, who told them that he had not seen her since she was 6 months old. Mr. Bessant was aghast because he had questioned his wife numerous times about the pediatrician's opinion of Rinna's development. The pediatrician referred the family to the state medical university 200 miles away where Rinna received a comprehensive evaluation and a diagnosis of emotional disturbance. Mr. Bessant was overcome with guilt when the psychologist informed him of Rinna's description of life under the care of her mother. He feels that he is responsible for Rinna's condition since he did not get her the proper care she needed. The evaluation team at the hospital recommended that Rinna attend the residential psychiatric kindergarten school program at the hospital, where she would have the benefits of an intensive treatment plan that would not be possible in other settings. Both Mr. Bessant and his mother were adamant in their feeling that Rinna needed to come home to be cared for, so they could try to make up for the past neglect. They feel that given time and lots of loving care, Rinna will once again become "well."

Case Study Activity

INDIVIDUAL OR GROUP CASE ANALYSIS

Answer the following questions and be prepared to discuss them in class.

1. Does Rinna's diagnosis of emotional disturbance influence the type of methods that Mrs. Vasquez will use to teach her readiness skills? Why or why not?

_____

_____

_____

_____

_____

_____

_____

_____

2. What can Mrs. Vasquez do about Rinna's classroom behavior? Describe two possible behavior management plans that could be used in this situation.

_____

_____

_____

_____

_____

_____

_____

_____

3. While Mrs. Vasquez is working on a plan for Rinna's behavior, what can she do to help the other children to adjust to the classroom situation?

_____

_____

_____

_____

_____

_____

_____

4. What resources could Mrs. Vasquez use to assist her with this student? Name at least three.

_____

_____

_____

_____

_____

_____

_____

_____

5. Does Rinna belong in Mrs. Vasquez's kindergarten class? Does she belong in the psychiatric kindergarten at the state hospital? Support your opinion for the most appropriate placement for this child.

_____

_____

_____

_____

_____

_____

_____

_____

6. How would you handle the kindergarten parents' complaints about Rinna? What would you tell the principal regarding this situation?

_____

_____

_____

_____

_____

_____

_____

7. Describe two long-term goals for Rinna's behavior that should be included in her IEP. Specify four short-term goals for each of these.

_____

_____

_____

_____

_____

_____

_____

_____

8. How could the special education teacher, Mr. Asante, be more helpful in this situation? Give three possible suggestions.

_____

_____

_____

_____

_____

_____

_____

_____

9. What do you think is the long-term prognosis for this child? What factors could increase the chances of a more favorable prognosis? What factors would adversely affect the outcome for Rinna?

_____

_____

_____

_____

_____

_____

_____

_____

Serena

Serena is a 16-year-old senior at Newman High School. She has recently returned from a year's stay at a residential school that specializes in the treatment of adolescents with mental illness. Serena was being treated for anxiety reaction and bulimia. Although the residential school recommended that Serena spend the next 2 years there, Serena's parents, Mr. and Mrs. Kendall, wanted their daughter at home. Mr. and Mrs. Kendall have spoken with the principal, Mrs. Wojak, about Serena's emotional problems, particularly her anxiety attacks. Although it is their feeling that Serena is "cured," they have asked the principal to keep a watchful eye on her and to inform her teachers about her emotional difficulties. They are particularly concerned about her speech class, which is a graduation requirement at Newman. Public speaking has been the source of numerous panic attacks in the past, and they want the teacher to be advised of this potential problem. Mrs. Wojak has assured Mr. and Mrs. Kendall that Serena will do fine.

Background Information:

Serena's emotional problems were first noted by her kindergarten teacher, who felt that Serena was the shyest child she had ever seen in kindergarten. She shared these concerns at two parent–teacher conferences she had with the Kendalls. By the time Serena got to second grade, her teacher had decided to refer her for special education evaluation. He was concerned about her "nervousness and tendency to cry at the drop of a hat." In third grade, the pupil assessment team had adequate observational data to recommend that Serena receive some help for an emotional disturbance, which was identified as anxiety withdrawal. The Kendalls declined placement because they did not agree with the evaluation report. They felt that the assessment team was confusing a natural tendency to be shy with pathological behavior.

Serena's problems continued to worsen as she grew older. However, the school stopped pursuing placement because the parents were resolved in their decision not to have her identified as a special education student. When Serena was 13, she began to lose weight in a drastic manner. At about the same time, she began having severe stomachaches. Her mother began to observe her carefully and discovered Serena's binge and purge cycles. She took her to the pediatrician who recommended a psychologist. Serena saw this same psychologist for 2 years without any sign of recovery. In fact, Serena's condition deteriorated. Shortly after Mrs. Kendall discovered the bulimia, Serena began having full-blown panic attacks. These panic attacks appeared to be related to performance-type activities such as giving an oral book report, playing a flute solo in band, or participating in volleyball tournaments. Serena began dropping out of extracurricular activities that required her to perform in public. She begged her mother to talk to her teachers so she could be excused from any type of class presentation. Mrs. Kendall reluctantly agreed because she didn't know what else to do.

Finally Serena's pediatrician recommended that she be hospitalized. He felt that Serena's condition was becoming life threatening. The pediatrician, with the help of the psychologist, found a residential school that specialized in eating disorders, among other types of mental illness. Serena hated the school, but eventually accepted her treatment when her parents promised her that she could leave after the academic year. When the school released Serena to Mr. and Mrs. Kendall, they made it clear that Serena was still having problems with anxiety and eating. The Kendalls told school officials that they planned to have Serena resume treatment from the psychologist she had been seeing before she entered residential treatment.

Case Study Activity

INDIVIDUAL OR GROUP CASE ANALYSIS

Answer the following questions and be prepared to discuss them in class.

1. Do you think that Serena should be receiving special education services at the secondary level? Why or why not?

_____

_____

_____

_____

_____

_____

_____

2. Why do you think that Serena's parents have not allowed her to receive special education services in the past? Do you agree or disagree with their reasoning?

_____

_____

_____

_____

_____

_____

_____

3. Do you think that the services of the psychologist are a good substitute for the special education services Serena would have received in school? Explain your answer.

_____

_____

_____

_____

_____

4. If you were Serena's parent, would you have kept her in the residential school in spite of her objections? Why or why not?

_____

5. What should Mrs. Wojak do with the information she now has about Serena?

_____

6. If you were Serena's speech teacher, how would you modify your class to increase the possibility that she will be able to achieve the objectives?

_____

_____

_____

_____

_____

7. What would you do if you were Serena's teacher, and you were told by a student that she was throwing up in the restroom?

_____

_____

_____

_____

_____

_____

_____

_____

_____

Physical Needs

CHAPTER 5

Chad

Chad is a 12-year-old sixth grader at Daniels Middle School. He was diagnosed with acute lymphoblastic leukemia at the age of 7. Since this time he has been in and out of remission. He has recently had a relapse that required intensive chemotherapy and caused him to lose all of his hair. Chad has mild learning disabilities in the areas of reading and math. He also struggles with subtle language processing difficulties and problems with short term memory. It is believed that these learning problems are related to the intensive chemotherapy that he has endured to combat the cancer. Mr. Chong, his English teacher, has previously been concerned about Chad's achievement, but he has started to become more concerned about Chad's withdrawn behavior. Chad has stopped participating in class, and he is not doing any homework. He generally keeps his head down on the desk during English class or stares out the window. When Mr. Chong tries to include him in discussion, he seldom answers but just shrugs his shoulders, keeping his eyes fixed on his shoes.

Mr. Chong has shared his concern with Mrs. Hafstrom, Chad's learning disabilities teacher. Mrs. Hafstrom is also worried about Chad. During the 50 minutes per day that he attends her learning lab, he seems distant and preoccupied. Mrs. Hafstrom believes that he is very depressed about his illness. When she questions him about how he's feeling, he frequently makes off-hand remarks, such as, "Pretty good for a kid who's headed for the grave," or "I'm feeling kind of down, like six feet under." This kind of talk alienates Chad from his peers, who more and more frequently are avoiding him. Mrs. Hafstrom believes that Chad is a very depressed child who needs help, but she is uncertain of how to go about providing this assistance to him.

Background Information:

During the last IEP meeting, Mrs. Hafstrom requested that Chad be invited to participate in setting goals. Chad's mother, Mrs. Kelly, told her that his inclusion was "absolutely out of the question." At the meeting, Mr. and Mrs. Kelly told the pupil assessment team that they did not want Chad to be present because they wanted to talk about the prognosis of his illness. They related how Chad's oncologist had told them that Chad would probably die sometime this year. His doctor believes that there will not be another remission of the cancer. Mrs. Kelly tearfully told the team that she wanted Chad to have the best year possible without him having to worry about the seriousness of his illness. In spite of the doctor's recommendation that Chad be informed of the prognosis, Mr. and Mrs. Kelly believe that no purpose can be served by giving him this information. It was obvious to all the assessment team members who were present that both parents were in such a state of grief that they could not look at other alternatives for helping Chad face his illness. At the close of the IEP meeting, Mrs. Kelly made it clear that she did not want any teacher or psychologist to discuss the issue of death with Chad. Both parents insisted that the IEP goals should address only academic needs and the family would deal with the affective needs.

Case Study Activity

INDIVIDUAL OR GROUP CASE ANALYSIS

Answer the following questions and be prepared to discuss them in class.

1. Do you think that Chad knows what his prognosis is? Why or why not? Should he be told? Explain your position.

_____

_____

_____

_____

_____

_____

2. If you were Mrs. Hafstrom would you attempt to change the parents' minds about informing Chad of his prognosis? Explain your position.

_____

_____

_____

_____

_____

_____

3. If you were Mr. Chong, what would you do in English class to increase Chad's participation?

_____

_____

_____

_____

_____

_____

4. If you were Mrs. Hafstrom, how would you help meet Chad's affective needs given the restrictions the parents have placed on you?

_____

_____

_____

_____

_____

_____

_____

5. Should students with disabilities typically be present at their IEP meetings, or is it a good idea to exclude them, particularly when information of a sensitive nature is going to be discussed? Explain your position.

_____

_____

_____

_____

_____

_____

_____

6. As a teacher, can you think of any other ways you might be able to assist this family?

_____

_____

_____

_____

_____

_____

_____

Denisa

Denisa is a 7-year-old student in the first grade at Cherry Ridge Elementary. At the age of 3, she was identified as having developmental disabilities and was placed in a noncategorical preschool program. After 3 years in this program, Denisa was placed in a self-contained special education primary classroom. This year is Denisa's first year in a regular education classroom. Her teacher, Mrs. Estrada, is anxious about having Denisa in her classroom. At the beginning of the year, the principal told the faculty that a student with AIDS would be entering Cherry Ridge. Privacy laws prevented him from identifying the student, so he advised all teachers to use precautions, as if that student were in each classroom. As the faculty talked among themselves, they identified a handful of possible students who might be the one with AIDS. In Mrs. Estrada's class, there is one child, Denisa, who stands out as a very sickly child and who is noticeably frail when compared to the other students. Mrs. Estrada also knows that Denisa's mother has had several drug-related convictions and that her father died last year from an unspecified illness.

Mrs. Estrada likes to think of herself as a fair-minded person who is not prejudiced against others. However, she has admitted to herself that she is frightened by this child, and she wishes desperately that Denisa had ended up in someone else's classroom. She knows that Denisa needs a lot of help, especially with her reading and math, but she is hesitant to work with her on a one-to-one basis or to assign a peer tutor to her. She's not even sure that Denisa should be included in cooperative learning activities. Mrs. Estrada is considering asking the principal to put her in a self-contained special education classroom on the basis of her academic needs.

Background Information:

Mrs. Estrada is correct. Denisa is the child with AIDS to whom the principal was referring. Denisa was infected in utero as her mother, Mrs. Diaz, was an intravenous drug user. Denisa has had developmental and medical problems since her birth. She has been in the hospital over a half a dozen times in the last 5 years for serious, life-threatening infections.

Denisa's father died of AIDS last year, and there is a good possibility that Mrs. Diaz will die before the end of this year. She is trying to hang on as long as possible for the benefit of Denisa, but the disease is rapidly taking its course. The mother is desperately worried about who will care for her child when she is gone. Her family has disowned her, and her husband's family will not speak to her as they believe she is responsible for encouraging their son's drug use.

Mrs. Diaz is also trying to make amends for infecting Denisa. She has devoted all of her remaining energy to taking care of this child and trying to make sure that she gets everything she needs. She has been to the school three times since the beginning of the year to talk to Mrs. Estrada about Denisa's academic progress. Mrs. Diaz has wanted to confide in her about Denisa's AIDS, but she is unsure about whether she should do this. She did tell Mrs. Estrada that she was a past drug user and that she has changed her life mainly for her daughter. She wanted her to know how much she cared for Denisa and how important it was for her to be a good mother. She also told Mrs. Estrada that if there were anything she could do at home to help Denisa's academic work, she would be more than willing to do it.

 Case Study Activity

INDIVIDUAL OR GROUP CASE ANALYSIS

Answer the following questions and be prepared to discuss them in class.

1. Why can't the principal of this school identify the student with AIDS? Do you think that teachers should be provided with this information? Why or why not?

_____

_____

_____

_____

_____

_____

_____

2. What is the relationship between AIDS and learning problems?

_____

_____

_____

_____

_____

_____

_____

3. What should Mrs. Estrada do about her difficulty accepting this student? Are there specific resources available that might help her?

_____

_____

_____

_____

_____

_____

_____

4. If you were Mrs. Estrada, would you recommend that Denisa be placed in a self-contained special education classroom? Why or why not?

_____

_____

_____

_____

_____

_____

_____

5. Should Denisa be assigned a peer tutor? Do you think it is a good idea for her to participate in cooperative learning activities? Explain your responses.

_____

_____

_____

_____

_____

_____

_____

_____

6. What will probably happen to Denisa when her mother dies?

_____

_____

_____

_____

_____

_____

_____

_____

7. Should Mrs. Estrada try to develop a tutoring program for Mrs. Diaz to use with Denisa at home? Why or why not? If you think this is a good idea, explain the type of program that might work well in this situation.

_____

_____

_____

_____

_____

_____

_____

_____

_____

8. Is Mrs. Estrada at risk for contracting AIDS from Denisa or her mother? Are Denisa's peers at risk? Why or why not?

_____

_____

_____

_____

_____

_____

_____

_____

_____

Jamal

Jamal is a 10-year-old fifth grader at Lawton Elementary School. Three months ago, he was hit by a car while running across a busy street with a group of older children. He spent 2 months recuperating at a children's hospital and 1 month at home. This week he will be returning to school where he will be in Mr. Iskra's regular fifth-grade class for most of the instructional day. He will be going to a special education learning lab for an hour and a half each day to work with Mrs. Kramer. Jamal's teachers have been told that his speech and language will be quite limited for some time as a result of his accident. He has approximately 50 words in his vocabulary, but he is showing good progress since the accident. His teachers have also been told that he is working on a preacademic basis. He does not have the visual–motor skills necessary to write legibly. He is learning the alphabet, and he knows number concepts through 6. Although Jamal's physical therapist expects him to walk eventually, at this point he is using a wheelchair.

In addition to Jamal's learning problems, he is also experiencing some behavioral difficulties. The records from the hospital describe Jamal as "irritable and combative." He regularly refused to work with some of his therapists and would throw objects at them to get them to leave him alone. The hospital has recommended that the school develop a structured behavior management plan to assist Jamal in his anger control.

Background Information:

School records indicate that Jamal had a number of behavioral problems prior to his accident. He was frequently in trouble for fighting and being disrespectful to his teachers. Jamal has been described by former teachers as being "quick to anger" and "reacting aggressively to the least provocation." Jamal was abandoned by his parents when he was 2 years old. He lives with his 87-year-old grandmother who cannot come to school because of health problems. In the past, when she has been contacted about Jamal's behavior, she has told the school that she rarely sees him and, when she does, he refuses to talk to her about school complaints. Since the accident, he appears to be even more angry and frustrated.

Case Study Activity

INDIVIDUAL OR GROUP CASE ANALYSIS

Answer the following questions and be prepared to discuss them in class.

1. Should Jamal be placed in a regular education classroom? Why or why not?

_____

_____

_____

_____

_____

_____

_____

2. What resources can Mr. Iskra use to prepare himself to work with Jamal? Name at least four different resources and explain why these might be effective.

_____

_____

_____

_____

_____

_____

_____

3. What strategies could Jamal's teachers use to help Jamal control his anger and frustration? Describe a behavior management plan that uses these strategies.

_____

_____

_____

_____

_____

_____

_____

4. How can Mrs. Kramer and Mr. Iskra work with Jamal's grandmother to establish continuity between the school and home environments? What obstacles would need to be addressed?

_____

_____

_____

_____

_____

_____

5. How could Mr. Iskra adapt the fifth-grade language arts curriculum for Jamal's needs? Give an example of a typical fifth-grade language arts lesson with a specific objective. Describe how this lesson could be modified to meet Jamal's educational needs. Your response should indicate specifically what Jamal would be expected to do and how his work would be evaluated.

_____

_____

_____

_____

_____

_____

_____

Janell

Janell is a 10-year-old child in the fourth grade at Wheeling Elementary School. She uses a wheelchair because she is paralyzed from the lumbar region down as a result of spina bifida. Janell also has learning disabilities that her doctor believes are the result of hydrocephalus, a condition with which she was born. Janell's brain was shunted immediately after her birth, and she has not experienced problems since that time. She is in a regular education classroom for the entire day, but she receives reading assistance from a special education teacher, Mrs. Kirchmar, who works with her for 30 minutes per day in her regular education classroom. Janell has recurrent seizures which are controlled by Dilantin. She experiences swollen and bleeding gums as a side effect of this medication. Janell has vision problems, including strabismus and refractive errors that require very thick lenses. Although she has had three eye surgeries, the strabismus is still readily apparent.

Janell has considerable difficulty with her school work, but both her fourth-grade and special education teachers are very supportive. They have recently become increasingly concerned because Janell appears to be becoming more and more withdrawn. She doesn't seem to have any friends and lately Mrs. Bowman, her regular education teacher, has noticed that she is becoming the object of classroom jokes. Many of these jokes are focused on her physical appearance, such as her crossed eyes, her weight (Janell weighs 130 pounds), and even her wheelchair. Mrs. Bowman is starting to think that maybe Janell would be happier in a special education setting where "she could be friends with other children who are confined to wheelchairs." Mrs. Kirchmar does not agree that a special education classroom is the answer for Janell, but she does agree that Janell is unhappy in her current school situation. Both teachers have attempted to get Mr. Metz, Janell's father, to come to school for a parent–teacher conference to discuss these concerns, but he has politely declined on numerous occasions. Finally, out of frustration, Mrs. Bowman and Mrs. Kirchmar went to see Mr. Metz at home in the evening. Mr. Metz would not let the teachers come into his home. He stood at the door and stated that he was not interested in discussing any of Janell's school difficulties because he had made the decision to place her in Roseman School, a residential school that serves children with severe disabilities. It has a reputation as a dismal institution where children are typically neglected. Both teachers were shocked to hear this news. When Mrs. Kirchmar asked him if they could come in just for a few minutes to talk about Roseman, Mr. Metz said, "No, I'm sorry—there's nothing more to talk about."

Background Information:

Janell's father is a widower whose wife died of cancer when Janell was 3 years old. Since that time, Mr. Metz has relied on an elderly neighbor to assist him in the care of Janell. This woman, Miss Shaw, has taken on all of the major responsibilities for this child. Miss Shaw buys Janell's clothes, dresses her, makes all of her meals for her, and helps her with homework and school projects. Miss Shaw is the family's only outside contact as they live a reclusive life. Miss Shaw comes over to Janell's house at 7:00 every morning when Mr. Metz leaves for work and stays until 8:00 in the evening when he returns. This routine continued for 7 years until last month when Miss Shaw fell as she was lifting Janell from her bed into her wheelchair. She broke her hip bone and ended up in the hospital. Miss Shaw's relatives have informed Mr. Metz that she will not be returning to her home because she will be living in a retirement home when she gets out of the hospital.

 Case Study Activities

PART I:
ROLE PLAYING

Break into groups of three and simulate a conference in which Janell's needs are addressed. Assume one of the following roles: Mrs. Bowman, Mrs. Kirchmar, and Mr. Gates, the school social worker. In a role-playing activity, the group should attempt to develop strategies for involving Mr. Metz and resolving this problem. Write a summary of the resolution.

Resolution

_____

_____

_____

_____

_____

_____

_____

_____

PART II:
INDIVIDUAL OR GROUP CASE ANALYSIS

Answer the following questions and be prepared to discuss them in class.

1. What do you think is the reason for Janell's withdrawal?

_____

_____

_____

_____

_____

_____

2. Why do you think that Mr. Metz refused to come to school for a conference? Do you think it was a good idea for Janell's teachers to make a home visit? Explain your answer. Are there other strategies that teachers can use to communicate with parents who are difficult to reach?

_____

_____

_____

_____

_____

_____

_____

3. Why would Janell's father want to put his daughter in a residential school that serves children with severe physical and mental disabilities?

_____

_____

_____

_____

_____

_____

4. Why do you think that Mrs. Bowman believes that Janell would be happier in a special education placement? Do you agree or disagree? Explain your position.

5. Is there anything that these teachers can do to stop Mr. Metz from putting Janell in this residential school?

6. If you were Mrs. Bowman, what would you do to increase Janell's socialization opportunities in the regular classroom? How would you deal with the jokes that are made by her peers?

Melissa

Melissa is a 13-year-old student in the eighth grade at Spencer Middle School. She is a very attractive adolescent who has been enormously popular among students and teachers alike since she started here in sixth grade. Last summer Melissa was involved in a bicycle accident that resulted in a closed head injury. Although Melissa is progressing very well considering the injury, her family has been told that it will take quite a while for her to fully recover. The doctors have also mentioned the possibility that Melissa may never have the same motor coordination that she had possessed prior to the accident. The most pressing concern for the family now is dealing with Melissa's seizure disorder, which has developed as a result of the head injury. Melissa now experiences tonic-clonic seizures on a weekly basis. Although a number of medications have been tried, they have not yet successfully controlled her seizures. Melissa's doctors hope that they will eventually be able to control these seizures, but, for the time being, they have told the family that they must be prepared to deal with them as they occur.

Melissa's parents, Mr. and Mrs. Zemke, have been working with the staff at Spencer to assure that Melissa's needs are accommodated. Initially they felt the school was very responsive to their requests, but lately they have had second thoughts. They are starting to wonder if they should hire an attorney to impress upon the school the necessity of the modifications they have requested. The major disagreement that has arisen is a result of differences regarding seizure management. Melissa's neurologist has emphasized the importance of preventing any secondary brain damage that might result from a fall during a seizure. The Zemkes have asked that Melissa's peers be trained in seizure management so that when Melissa starts to have a seizure, her peers can catch her and prevent her from hitting her head on a desk or the floor. The school does not agree with this request. The principal, Mrs. Gust, on the advice of the school nurse has recommended that Melissa wear a helmet during the day to protect her head in case of a fall from a seizure. When Mrs. Zemke heard this, she literally hit the roof. The idea of her daughter wearing a helmet around school all day, calling attention to her problems, was simply ludicrous to her.

Mrs. Gust has argued that it doesn't seem reasonable to expect Melissa's peers to be responsible for preventing secondary brain damage. She mentioned to the Zemkes that Melissa has gained a good deal of weight since the accident and that many of her peers could not physically catch her and keep her from hitting the floor. Mrs. Gust also brought up the subject of school liability. She noted that it was in the school district's best interests, as well as Melissa's, to use the best means of protection, and that, in the opinion of school health care professionals, was a helmet. Mrs. Zemke was already boiling at the idea of the helmet, but when Mrs. Gust mentioned Melissa's weight gain, she really got angry. She told Mrs. Gust that she was the most insensitive person that she had ever met, and that Melissa would never step foot in this school with a helmet on her head. She further stated that she did not know how Mrs. Gust became a middle school principal when it was obvious that she did not know anything about psychological development at this stage. Mr. Zemke tried to get his wife to calm down, but the discussion between the principal and Mrs. Zemke continued to escalate.

Mr. Zemke suggested another meeting to resolve these differences. They had yet to work out other issues that concerned the precipitation of Melissa's seizures. Many of the seizures appear to be triggered by visual stimulation. In Melissa's case, the flickering of fluorescent lights and visual patterns that have horizontal and vertical lines crossing, such as window panes and plaids, seem to be precipitants to seizure activity. The Zemkes had asked Mrs. Gust to request that all of Melissa's teachers avoid wearing plaids and to make sure that the blinds were pulled down in all of her classrooms so that she would not be exposed to the window pane configuration. Although Mrs. Gust did not turn down those requests, the Zemkes had the impression that she was resistant to making these modifications.

Background Information:

Prior to the bicycle accident, Melissa was a cheerleader and winner of the local Junior Miss competition, in which she chose dance as her area of talent. Since the accident, Melissa has not regained her gross or fine motor skills. She had to drop off the cheerleading squad, and she no longer dances. Her recuperation required a lengthy period of hospitalization in which she was bedridden. As a result of this inactivity, she has gained over 30 pounds. This weight gain has caused additional self-concept problems that Melissa is strug- gling to overcome. Her mother is particularly sensitive to comments about Melissa's new appearance because she knows it is a source of depression for Melissa, and it is also a reminder to Mrs. Zemke that she has lost the daughter she had before the head injury.

 ## Case Study Activities

PART I:
ROLE PLAYING

Break into groups of four and assume one of the following roles: Mrs. Gust, Ms. Sheldon (the school nurse), Mr. Zemke, and Mrs. Zemke. Simulate a problem-solving session in which the participants attempt to resolve this issue of seizure management for Melissa. Following the role-playing activity, provide a writ- ten summary of the resolution.

Resolution

_____

_____

_____

_____

_____

_____

_____

_____

_____

_____

_____

PART II:
INDIVIDUAL OR GROUP CASE ANALYSIS

Answer the following questions and be prepared to discuss them in class.

1. Does the school have the legal right to make Melissa wear a helmet during the school day? Why or why not? Do the parents have the legal right to specify how Melissa's teachers should dress?

_____

_____

_____

_____

_____

_____

_____

2. To what does the term "secondary brain damage" refer? Do you think that Melissa should wear a helmet to prevent secondary brain injury from falling as a result of a seizure?

_____

_____

_____

_____

_____

_____

3. What is a tonic-clonic seizure? Describe the characteristics of this form of seizure activity. What types of medication are typically used to control this type of seizure? Can these seizures be precipitated by the flickering of lights and certain visual patterns?

_____

_____

_____

_____

_____

_____

4. Do you agree with the Zemkes' suggestions for seizure management, that is, having the other students be responsible for catching Melissa? Why or why not?

_____

_____

_____

_____

_____

_____

_____

_____

5. Was it insensitive of Mrs. Gust to bring up the topic of Melissa's weight gain? Do you think that Mrs. Zemke overreacted to references to Melissa's weight?

_____

_____

_____

_____

_____

_____

_____

6. Do you have any other ideas for preventing secondary brain injury in Melissa's situation?

_____

_____

_____

_____

_____

_____

_____

7. If you were one of Melissa's teachers, how would you feel about dress modifications and keeping the blinds pulled down to assist this student? Explain your answer.

_____

_____

_____

_____

_____

_____

_____

Michael

Michael is an 8-year-old second grader at Port Andrew Elementary School. He was diagnosed with osteogenesis imperfecta (brittle bone disease) 2 years ago. Michael's teacher, Mrs. Briggs, does not feel that Michael's needs can be met in the regular classroom setting. She referred him to the pupil assessment team for special education testing. Mrs. Briggs has told the principal that she will transfer to another school unless Michael is removed from her classroom. She does not feel that teachers should be responsible for the physical needs of a child.

The assessment team report indicated that Michael's IQ fell into the bright average range, and his academic achievement was consistent with that finding. During the staffing, Michael's parents, Mr. and Mrs. Sampson, were stunned when the team members recommended that Michael be placed in the Wellington School, a special education school that serves students with severe cognitive and physical needs. The assessment team told the parents that because of Michael's fragile medical condition, his needs could not be met in the regular classroom. The team further suggested to the parents that they would not be responsible for Michael's health and safety if he remained in Port Andrew or any other regular education school in the district. Mr. and Mrs. Sampson have some familiarity with Wellington as a friend of theirs was an aide there for a number of years. They know that most of the students are severely or profoundly retarded and have extensive support needs. They cannot imagine that the assessment team thinks that this is an appropriate placement for their child.

Background Information:

During his kindergarten and first-grade years, Michael broke both of his legs, his arm, his ankle, and his wrist. He was diagnosed with osteogenesis imperfecta during the first grade. His first-grade teacher, Mrs. Lachman, felt that it was very stressful to have Michael in her classroom because she was so fearful that he would be injured. She referred him for special education evaluation, but Michael's parents refused to sign the papers. Mr. and Mrs. Sampson could not understand the purpose of the evaluation. They were also facing quite a bit of stress at that time because they were suspected of child abuse. Before the diagnosis of osteogenesis imperfecta, Michael's pediatrician was suspicious that a seemingly healthy child could have so many fractures, and so he reported the Sampsons for investigation of possible child abuse. When the diagnosis was made, it became clear to all parties that the parents were not involved in any wrongdoing, but Mr. and Mrs. Sampson never forgot the accusation and the fact that they had almost lost their son.

Mrs. Lachman spoke often of the need to get this child into a safer type of environment. Some of this conversation took place in the faculty lounge. When Mrs. Briggs found out she was going to have Michael in her classroom, she consulted with Mrs. Lachman who told her in no uncertain terms that Michael did not belong in a regular classroom. She said that Mrs. Briggs would be a nervous wreck trying to make sure that Michael wasn't injured in the course of the daily routine. She convinced Mrs. Briggs that Michael needed to be evaluated by the pupil assessment team in order to get him into another school. Mrs. Briggs, in turn, convinced the Sampsons to sign the papers for the evaluation by telling them that it was the only way the school could identify how to meet Michael's educational needs. The parents signed the papers just because they wanted to pacify Mrs. Briggs. They wanted to be sure that they started the school year off on the right foot. They felt they had not had a very good relationship with Mrs. Lachman, which, of course, adversely affected the way Michael felt about school last year.

 Case Study Activities

PART I:
ROLE PLAYING

Break into groups of four or five. Assume one of the following roles: Mr. Sampson, Mrs. Sampson, Mr. Landis (pupil assessment team coordinator), Mrs. Briggs, and Mrs. Lachman (an optional role). Simulate a problem-solving session in which the participants attempt to resolve the issues of educational placement and modifications for Michael. Following the role-playing activity, write a summary of the resolution.

Resolution

_____

_____

_____

_____

_____

_____

_____

_____

PART II:
INDIVIDUAL OR GROUP CASE ANALYSIS

Answer the following questions and be prepared to discuss them in class.

1. From a legal perspective, does the school have the right to assume this position regarding Michael's placement? Why or why not? What laws might influence this case?

_____

_____

_____

_____

_____

_____

_____

_____

2. Do you think that the Wellington School is appropriate for Michael's educational needs? Why or why not?

_____

_____

_____

_____

_____

_____

_____

_____

3. Describe four modifications of the regular classroom that could be made for Michael.

_____

_____

_____

_____

_____

_____

_____

_____

4. Do you think that Mrs. Lachman and Mrs. Briggs are overreacting? Explain your position. Do you think most teachers would hold this view of Michael?

_____

_____

_____

_____

_____

_____

_____

_____

5. If you were Michael's parent, what would you do about this situation?

_____

_____

_____

_____

_____

_____

_____

_____

6. Should Michael's parents fight to keep him in a classroom where the teacher clearly does not want him? Why or why not?

_____

_____

_____

_____

_____

_____

_____

Nicole

Nicole is a 5-year-old child who will be attending Hinckley Elementary School in a couple of months. For the past 2 years, Nicole has been in a special education preschool program. Nicole has cerebral palsy, which affects all four limbs to the extent that she requires a wheelchair for mobility. The pupil assessment team believes that she is severely retarded, but there is still some question about cognitive ability because she is nonverbal. The cerebral palsy has resulted in paralysis of the vocal folds. The assessment team feels that the extent of her cognitive disability will become more clear as Nicole develops.

Nicole's mother, Mrs. Buras, wants her to attend a regular kindergarten class in her own neighborhood. The school district would rather have Nicole spend another year in the special education preschool program, which is located at a school about 10 miles away. The special education director thinks that the most appropriate education for Nicole would include intensive physical, occupational, and speech–language therapies. This is the focus of the curriculum in the special education preschool setting. She has told Mrs. Buras that if Nicole is in the regular kindergarten, she will not be able to achieve many of the objectives that the other children will be working toward because of her communication and physical limitations. In addition to this concern, the special education director has also told Mrs. Buras that there will be no aide in the kindergarten class this year because of funding problems. Therefore, Nicole will, in all probability, not get the attention she needs. The kindergarten teacher, Mrs. Pekarus, does not see how she will manage 24 kindergartners without an aide, particularly with the addition of a multiply handicapped child, which would give her 25 students in all. After numerous meetings, it has been decided that Nicole will go to a regular kindergarten class, but only if Mrs. Buras can attend with her to help out. Mrs. Buras is elated when the decision is reached. She really feels that this is the kind of environment that will stimulate Nicole to acquire new skills.

Three weeks into the kindergarten year, Mrs. Buras is starting to feel the strain of her new schedule. She is having a difficult time keeping up with her responsibilities to her three other children as well as being with Nicole at school on a daily basis. When she brought this to Mrs. Pekarus's attention, the teacher remarked that everyone has to make difficult decisions, and she was sure that Nicole would be just as happy in the special education program if Mrs. Buras decided that was what she had to do. Mrs. Buras had been hoping that Mrs. Pekarus would respond by saying that she did not need to be there every day or that she now realized that Nicole was not the burden she had anticipated. She felt very dejected when she realized that 3 weeks with Nicole in the classroom had done nothing to change this teacher's mind. It was obvious that Mrs. Pekarus still did not want Nicole in her classroom.

Background Information:

Mrs. Buras has felt like she has been fighting the system ever since Nicole started in her preschool program. She knows that the special education personnel think that Nicole is severely or profoundly retarded, even though they readily admit that they do not have the appropriate tests to determine her potential. Mrs. Buras has the distinct impression that they have already decided that she will never communicate even though they talk a lot about the importance of language therapy. For a long time she has wanted to get her daughter out of the clutches of this special education team to see how she would function in a group of her peers. Mrs. Buras feels that being around children who are verbal may be much more stimulating than being in a special education classroom where no one talks except the therapists.

The special education director, pupil assessment team, and Mrs. Pekarus believe that Mrs. Buras has not accepted the fact that Nicole is severely retarded. They have spent considerable time as a group talking about how to assist this mother in shifting from her current stage of denial into a more realistic state of acceptance of the disability. They feel that once Mrs. Buras has accepted the extent of the disability, she will be in a position to more rationally discuss the necessity of specialized services for Nicole.

 ## Case Study Activity

INDIVIDUAL OR GROUP CASE ANALYSIS

Answer the following questions and be prepared to discuss them in class.

1. Do you think that Mrs. Buras is in a state of denial regarding her daughter's disability? Why or why not? Is it possible that the assessment team is wrong about Nicole's mental retardation? Explain your answer.

_____

_____

_____

_____

_____

_____

2. What is your opinion regarding the most appropriate placement for Nicole? Provide support for your response. Why do you think that the school district is so intent on having this child in a segregated setting?

_____

_____

_____

_____

_____

_____

_____

3. Can the school district actually require Mrs. Buras to assist her daughter as a contingency for school attendance? Why or why not? Are there any laws that would influence this situation?

_____

_____

_____

_____

_____

_____

_____

_____

4. Is it possible that this child's needs could be accommodated in Mrs. Pekarus's classroom without the assistance of Mrs. Buras? Explain your answer.

_____

_____

_____

_____

_____

_____

_____

_____

5. If you were the kindergarten teacher, what would your position be with regard to having this child in your classroom? Why?

_____

_____

_____

_____

_____

_____

_____

6. Do you agree or disagree with Mrs. Buras's idea that interaction with Nicole's peers might be more stimulating than the speech–language therapy? Why ?

_____

_____

_____

_____

_____

_____

_____

Robert

Robert is a 16-year-old sophomore at Blue Springs High School. He was diagnosed as having cerebral palsy shortly after he turned 1 year of age. Although his legs are the most severely affected, he also has restricted movement on the right side of his upper body. The limited body movement he has is characterized by spasticity, and his speech is characterized by dysarthria, which interferes with intelligibility. This is Robert's second year at Blue Springs High. Last year his guidance counselor, Mr. Kelso, worked with Robert and his mother to carefully choose courses that would be appropriate for his interests and educational needs. Robert receives speech therapy three times per week, as well as the services of a physical therapist to assist him with mobility exercises. He does not require any academic assistance. His grades last year were all Bs and Cs. Mr. Kelso is responsible for coordinating Robert's IEP, which will include a transition plan this year.

Last year Robert wanted to take French, but Mr. Kelso talked him out of it. He didn't feel that Robert would be successful in that class because of his speech problems. This year Robert appears to be more determined to take French. His mother, Ms. Michaud, is supporting him. When Mr. Kelso went to talk with the French teacher, Mrs. Bourcier, he did not get a warm reception. She has seen Robert in the halls, so she is somewhat familiar with him. She told Mr. Kelso that it was absolutely out of the question for Robert to be in her class. When Ms. Michaud was told of the French teacher's position, she decided to talk to her in person. She approached Mrs. Bourcier in a very tactful manner, explaining to her that her son wanted to learn French more than any other subject, and she was sure he would do well in that class. Mrs. Bourcier told Ms. Michaud that it would not be possible to have "a student like that" in French class, and that "there are places in this school for students like your son." After many years of dealing with attitudes like Mrs. Bourcier's, Ms. Michaud has determined that the best way to respond to these situations is to calmly stand her ground, so she kept repeating, "Robert would really like to be in your class." Mrs. Bourcier continued to defend her position by saying, "Your son can't be in my class, because I can't understand what he's saying in English. How could I evaluate him in French?" and "It wouldn't be fair to him, he'll flunk." Ms. Michaud ended the conference by saying that Robert would look forward to studying with her. Mrs. Bourcier decided to let Mr. Kelso deal with this matter.

Meanwhile Mr. Kelso has been interviewing Robert with regard to his vocational interests so that a transition plan can be developed for him. Robert has told Mr. Kelso that he wants to be a commercial airline pilot, and he is not interested in learning any other skills in terms of a vocation. He has agreed to the community living skills program, which will include grocery shopping, checkbook balancing, and budgeting, but he doesn't want to be involved in any of the vocational programs. Robert wants to take all of the courses that are considered to be prerequisites for the college bound student. Mr. Kelso doesn't think this is a good idea, as he is sure that Robert is going to have considerable problems with many of those classes. He's also not sure how he should counsel Robert with regard to his flying ambitions. Ms. Michaud has indicated to Mr. Kelso that Robert is going through a sensitive period. He's feeling left out because he isn't getting his driver's license, dating, or participating in sports. She mentioned that she is also unsure of how to advise him on certain things because he has been "flying off the handle" a lot lately when she makes certain suggestions.

Another problem that has arisen for this student concerns Robert's use of a walker. Several of Robert's teachers have complained to Mr. Kelso that Robert is always late to class because it takes him so long to move from room to room. They feel that he would do better if he didn't miss the first 10 minutes of class. Two of these teachers have also complained that it is distracting to the other students to have Robert come in late and take an additional 5 minutes to struggle over to his seat. Mr. Kelso mentioned this to Robert's physical therapist, Mrs. Cox. She told Mr. Kelso that she has been recommending for some time now that Robert give up the walker for a wheelchair, but he refuses to follow this suggestion. Mrs. Cox feels that it is a sensitive topic for Robert at this stage in his development, so she hasn't pushed the issue.

Mr. Kelso has now realized that there are three important issues that he needs to resolve for this one student—enrolling in the French class, using the walker versus the wheelchair, and setting vocational goals. Since these issues involve the cooperation of different people, he's thinking that he should call a conference to discuss the situation. He likes Robert, and he hopes to help him work out some of these difficulties without hurting his feelings.

Background Information:

Robert's father was a Canadian Air Force pilot who married his mother when she was studying in Quebec. When Robert was diagnosed with cerebral palsy, the doctor painted a grim picture of all the things that Robert would never be able to do. This was apparently too much for his father to accept because he left the family shortly thereafter. Robert's mother stayed on in Quebec for a year after the divorce, hoping that Robert's father might show some interest in his son, but that was not to be the case. Robert's father never came back to visit his son after he had left. Ms. Michaud decided to return to the States where she would have the support of her family.

Although Robert's father has never contacted him, Robert is still very much aware of him. He keeps a framed picture of him on his bureau amidst the model airplanes that are part of his collection. He occasionally asks his mother for details about his father's life. Ms. Michaud has never hinted that his father could not accept Robert's disability, but she suspects that Robert understands the truth. Her greatest fear is that Robert will one day call him on the phone and that his father will hang up on him. What Ms. Michaud doesn't realize is that Robert has already done this. Mr. Michaud did hang up on Robert, but it was because he did not understand Robert's speech and thought it was a prank call.

 Case Study Activities

PART I:
ROLE PLAYING

Break into groups of five. Simulate a conference in which the three different issues facing this student are resolved. The following roles should be assumed: Robert, Mr. Kelso, Mrs. Cox, Ms. Michaud, and Mrs. Bourcier. Write a summary of the resolution, being sure to address each of the three issues.

Resolution

_____

_____

_____

_____

_____

_____

_____

_____

_____

_____

_____

_____

PART II:
INDIVIDUAL OR GROUP CASE ANALYSIS

Answer the following questions and be prepared to discuss them in class.

1. Do you think that Mr. Kelso should counsel Robert out of the idea of becoming a commercial airline pilot? Why or why not? Does Robert's disability preclude him from meeting the requirements for this profession? Explain your answer.

_____

_____

_____

_____

_____

_____

_____

2. Should Mrs. Bourcier allow Robert to take her French class? What do you think of her position that his speech problems would interfere with his ability to pass the class? Does the school have a right to exclude him from this class? What laws might influence this particular situation? Do you think that Robert can experience success in this class? Will he require modifications?

_____

_____

_____

_____

_____

_____

_____

3. Should Robert use a wheelchair instead of a walker? Why do you think he is resistant to the idea of giving up his walker? If he continues to use the walker, how can the problem of tardiness be alleviated?

_____

_____

_____

_____

_____

_____

_____

_____

4. Do you think that Robert's adolescent development has anything to do with his recent reactions to suggestions from his mother, guidance counselor, and teachers? Explain your answer. Are there any other factors in Robert's life that may be causing him to experience stress?

_____

_____

_____

_____

_____

_____

_____

_____

5. How could the school assist this family while they are working through a difficult time? Give three possible ways the school could be supportive of this adolescent and his mother.

_____

_____

_____

_____

_____

_____

_____

6. What is dysarthria and how is it related to cerebral palsy? What kind of cerebral palsy does Robert have? Is this a progressive disorder?

_____

_____

_____

_____

_____

_____

_____

_____

_____

Tom

Tom is a 14-year-old student at Lone Tree High School. He was diagnosed as having traumatic brain injury after an accident with a gun that occurred 6 months ago. Although he was previously in the National Honor Society, his pupil assessment team reports indicate that his IQ is now in the low 80s, and he has significant language deficits. He has been placed in Mr. Green's homeroom and English block. For the remainder of the day, he will receive special education services from Mrs. Evans, the learning disability teacher. Mr. Green has been told to expect Tom to have a great deal of difficulty adjusting to the classroom routine. His academic skills appear to be at approximately the fourth-grade level, with math being slightly higher than reading and written expression. Memory loss is presenting additional problems; for example, Tom has forgotten his multiplication tables and can't consistently remember the names of his peers. Mr. Green has also been informed that this adolescent is extremely depressed and has spoken frequently of suicide since the accident. His depression seems centered around the knowledge that there are so many things that he can't do now, things that were easy for him before.

In addition to the loss of academic skill, Tom has lost much of his athletic coordination. Although he can walk, he struggles with physical activities that require more coordination. Prior to the accident, Tom was a well-rounded athlete who excelled in baseball. He was the top player on the junior high team and had won many valuable player awards. Tom told his rehabilitation counselor that he is depressed over the loss of his athletic ability, but he is actually more frustrated about his intellectual and language problems. He has to struggle to put four or five words together to make a sentence. Oftentimes, he just gives up because it is too hard for him. When he experiences this frustration, he will throw things and use profanity. This behavior has further alienated him from his peers, and his friends are often fearful of him. Right after the accident, these friends provided Tom with a lot of support, but lately they have been steering clear of him because of his erratic behavior.

Background Information:

Tom had found the key to his father's gun cabinet and was showing a friend his father's guns when the accident occurred. His parents had strictly forbidden him to ever open that cabinet and had warned him time and time again that "guns are not toys." When the accident happened, Tom had been clowning around, simulating a game of Russian roulette. Notes from the social worker at the rehabilitation institute reveal that Tom's parents have not been able to let go of their anger. Other information from the social worker indicates that the parents, particularly the father, are having a difficult time accepting the fact that Tom will not be able to participate in athletics on a competitive basis. The father played baseball in the minor leagues for a number of years, and it appeared that Tom had the ability to do at least as well. Although his physical therapist feels that Tom has made remarkable progress (he had to learn to walk again), she has told the parents that it is unlikely that his coordination will ever be what it was before the accident.

 Case Study Activity

INDIVIDUAL OR GROUP CASE ANALYSIS

Answer the following questions and be prepared to discuss them in class.

1. What kinds of strategies could Mr. Green use to accommodate Tom's academic needs? Give five examples.

_____

_____

_____

_____

_____

_____

_____

_____

_____

_____

_____

_____

2. How should Mr. Green deal with Tom's behavioral outbursts in the classroom? Should this student be dismissed from class for the use of profanity? Describe the type of behavior management plan that Mr. Green could use for Tom's behavior.

_____

_____

_____

_____

_____

_____

_____

_____

_____

_____

_____

3. How can Mrs. Evans work with Mr. Green to help Tom be more successful and comfortable at school? Give four specific recommendations.

_____

_____

_____

_____

_____

_____

_____

_____

_____

4. What can be done to address this student's depression? Give four specific recommendations.

_____

_____

_____

_____

_____

_____

_____

_____

_____

_____

_____

5. How can Tom's teachers help him with his socialization problems?

_____

_____

_____

_____

_____

_____

_____

_____

6. How can the school help this family in dealing with this difficult adjustment period?

_____

_____

_____

_____

_____

_____

_____

_____

_____

_____

_____

Travis

Travis is a 4-year-old preschool student at Clarkson Elementary School. He had been adjusting well in his preschool program, but his teacher, Mrs. Ellsworth, started to notice that he was experiencing respiratory problems. These respiratory problems seemed to be associated with the cold viruses that continually make their way around the preschool class. Whenever Travis got a cold, Mrs. Ellsworth observed that he appeared to have a difficult time breathing, and he experienced significant coughing episodes. The preschool teacher called Travis's mother, Ms. Shoemacher, to have him picked up on several occasions because his breathing was so labored.

Last month Travis ended up in the hospital on oxygen because of a particularly severe upper respiratory virus that caused major breathing problems. When he came back to school Ms. Shoemacher brought a nebulizer and medication to be adminstered during the school day. Mrs. Ellsworth was caught off guard when she saw all the medical supplies—face mask, solution cup, saline solution to be measured and mixed with a prescription drug, and tubing for the machine. When Ms. Shoemacher started explaining the measurement, administration, and cleaning of equipment, Mrs. Ellsworth stopped her, saying, "Ms. Shoemacher, I am not a doctor or a nurse. I simply could not take the responsibility for giving this medical treatment to your son." Ms. Shoemacher seemed surprised and hurt by Mrs. Ellsworth's reaction. She told her that if she didn't agree to help with the treatment that Travis wouldn't be able to come to school. Mrs. Ellsworth apologized, but said that even though she had an aide, there was no way they had the time to stop the preschool activities for 16 children to provide this treatment for Travis. Ms. Shoemacher gathered up Travis and his equipment and quietly left the room without saying anything else. Mrs. Ellsworth could see that tears were running down her face. Travis was confused and upset. Mrs. Ellsworth felt terrible. But what else could she do?

Background Information:

Travis's preschool is a public school program administrated by the South County School District. The parents of the preschoolers pay the tuition that pays for the preschool teachers' salaries, while the school district provides the space and the materials for the program. It is an extended-day preschool with hours from 8 A.M. to 3 P.M.

Travis was diagnosed as having asthma at the age of 3. His mother has worked hard to minimize this con-dition so that Travis could have a normal childhood. Travis always had a nanny before he went to preschool, so she was able to provide him with the nebulizer treatments he needed. Last year Travis's father and mother were divorced and, since that time, Ms. Shoemacher has struggled financially. Mr. Shoemacher has paid sporadic child support, and he sees Travis about every other month. Travis and Ms. Shoemacher had to leave their home and move into an apartment when the bank foreclosed on the mortgage. Ms. Shoemacher also had to let the nanny go because she could no longer afford her. She put Travis in a home day-care situation, which lasted for about 6 months. The day-care provider started getting nervous about Travis' breathing. She finally told Ms. Shoemacher that she was getting too old to take on this kind of responsibility, and she could not take care of Travis any longer.

Ms. Shoemacher felt like she was at the end of her rope when she heard about the public preschool program in her school district. She arranged to have her work hours run from 8:30 to 2:30, with the provision that she take work home every evening to make up for the other 2 hours of the 8-hour work day. She was just starting to hope that things might work out for Travis and her. The emotional turmoil and stress caused by the recent events of the divorce, change in living arrangements, and trying to cover the hospital bills for Travis were starting to overwhelm her. She decided not to say anything to the preschool about Travis' condition, hoping that if she gave him a treatment in the morning, he would be able to make it through the rest of the day until she could pick him up in the afternoon and give him another treatment.

 ## Case Study Activity

INDIVIDUAL OR GROUP CASE ANALYSIS

Answer the following questions and be prepared to discuss them in class.

1. Should Ms. Shoemacher have told the school about Travis' asthma? Why or why not?

_____

_____

_____

_____

_____

_____

_____

_____

_____

2. Is it unreasonable to expect Mrs. Ellsworth or her aide to provide Travis with this treatment during school hours? Why or why not?

_____

_____

_____

_____

_____

_____

_____

_____

_____

_____

3. Does the school have a legal right to refuse to enroll Travis because of his medical condition? What laws could influence this situation?

_____

_____

_____

_____

_____

_____

_____

_____

_____

_____

4. What kind of preschool should Travis be in? Should Ms. Shoemacher be looking into schools that are associated with hospitals or the possibility of home schooling for Travis? Should she be pursuing placement in the regular public school classroom? Where can this child's needs be met?

_____

_____

_____

_____

_____

_____

_____

_____

5. It is obvious that Mrs. Ellsworth is an empathic teacher who is struggling with this problem. If you were this teacher, what would you do to resolve this situation?

_____

_____

_____

_____

_____

_____

_____

_____

_____

6. How far should schools be expected to go in terms of providing different treatments to meet the needs of children? Are there any court cases that have established precedents for these situations?

_____

_____

_____

_____

Communication Needs

CHAPTER 6

Hannah

Hannah is a 5-year-old kindergarten student at Winnetka Lake Elementary School. Mrs. Lindstrom, the kindergarten teacher, is very worried about Hannah's speech and language development. Hannah has been in her room for over a month now and has uttered less than five words the whole time. Mrs. Lindstrom referred her for a speech and language evaluation during the first week of the school year. The report from the pupil assessment team indicated that Hannah's speech and language development was well within the normal range, and that she was probably having a temporary adjustment problem that would take care of itself in the next couple of months. Mrs. Lindstrom was somewhat dismayed by the team's report because it was explained to her that since Hannah did not have a disability, no services would be available to her.

Winnetka Lake Elementary School is located in a very low socioeconomic area. Mrs. Lindstrom has 26 kindergartners who have a variety of different needs. She considers Hannah's problem to be pressing because it is greatly interfering with her socialization, an important objective for kindergarten. She has no friends whatsoever, and she does not participate in any oral activities. She feels that a child who doesn't speak should be getting some special services. It is very disturbing to her that the assessment team inferred that Hannah's language development was normal and did not require intervention.

Background Information:

Hannah did not attend preschool, so there is no information regarding the existence of this problem before kindergarten. When Mrs. Lindstrom called Hannah's mother, Mrs. Pappas, to discuss the problem, Mrs. Pappas just laughed and told Mrs. Lindstrom that Hannah "won't shut up at home." With that information, Mrs. Lindstrom felt more optimistic and decided to give Hannah some time for kindergarten adjustment. After 2 more weeks of total silence, Mrs. Lindstrom called Mrs. Pappas and asked her to come in for a conference. Mrs. Pappas declined saying it was the school's problem, so it was up to them to do something about it. Mrs. Pappas also requested that Mrs. Lindstrom not call her again about this problem. That is when Mrs. Lindstrom decided to refer Hannah for testing.

Permission to test was obtained through a home visit by the school social worker. After completing the testing, the report referred to Hannah's reluctance to speak as elective mutism and attributed it to an adjustment problem. The report suggested that there was not a significant problem at this time because achievement was within the low normal range, indicating that the child was learning. The only recommendation that the assessment team gave was that Hannah should be provided a warm and supportive learning environment so that she would be comfortable at school.

Case Study Activity

INDIVIDUAL OR GROUP CASE ANALYSIS

Answer the following questions and be prepared to discuss them in class.

1. Do you agree or disagree with the assessment team's opinion that Hannah does not require special education services at this time? Explain your answer.

_____

_____

_____

_____

_____

_____

_____

_____

2. If you were Mrs. Lindstrom, would you attempt to get Mrs. Pappas more involved in solving this problem? If yes, give two strategies that you might try to encourage her participation. If no, explain your position.

_____

_____

_____

_____

_____

_____

_____

_____

3. How could the assessment team have been more helpful in their evaluation of this child?

_____

_____

_____

_____

_____

_____

_____

4. Give four strategies that Mrs. Lindstrom could use for increasing Hannah's verbalization in the kindergarten classroom.

_____

_____

_____

_____

_____

_____

_____

5. Give four strategies that Mrs. Lindstrom could use for increasing socialization for this child.

_____

_____

_____

_____

_____

_____

_____

6. What resources might Mrs. Lindstrom use to help her work with Hannah?

_____

_____

_____

_____

_____

_____

Kayla

Kayla is a 4-year-old child at Cedar Point Elementary School. She is a student in Mrs. Chung's kindergarten classroom of 24 students. Kayla is a very bright little girl whose IQ falls in the gifted range. Although she will not turn 5 for another month, she is reading on the second-grade level. Math skills are considered to be somewhat lower, at approximately the mid first-grade level. Kayla has a severe speech impairment that significantly interferes with her communication. Her vocalizations are basically unintelligible to all except her family. When Kayla tries to speak, she is not able to articulate sounds in a typical fashion. Her speech is similar to that of a profoundly deaf individual who is not able to reproduce speech sounds.

Mrs. Chung understands very little of anything that Kayla says. The other kindergartners are also unable to comprehend her speech. This has created a very frustrating learning environment for this child, so that she resorts to temper tantrums when she cannot make her needs known. Kayla will pick up any nearby object—such as a book, pencil holder, globe, or chair—and hurl it as far as she can without regard for those who may be in the path of these objects. Kayla has been in Mrs. Chung's classroom for 3 weeks and, during this brief time, her mother has been called to the school over eight times to pick her up because of behavioral incidents. Mrs. Chung is very anxious about this situation. She is afraid that a student will be injured during one of Kayla's temper tantrums.

Kayla has speech therapy for 20 minutes per day with Ms. Gordon, the speech therapist. Mrs. Chung is grateful for this therapy because for 20 minutes Kayla will be out of the room, and she will be free to teach her students without fear of objects flying around the room. When Mrs. Chung told Ms. Gordon that she is having a difficult time with Kayla's behavior, she seemed understanding and gave her a book of behavior management strategies. Unfortunately Mrs. Chung hasn't had the opportunity to try any of these because Kayla ends up being sent home so frequently. She feels like she isn't making any progress whatsoever. Mrs. Chung is hesitant to go to the principal because she thinks he might infer that she can't manage her own class. This is Mrs. Chung's first year in the classroom, and she's starting to think that she should quit teaching and go to work for her father's travel agency.

Background Information:
Kayla's birth was a very difficult one. She was lodged in the birth canal for a long period of time before the obstetrician decided on a cesarean delivery. At the time of her birth, her Apgar was 5 at one minute and 6 at five minutes. Her pediatrician was very concerned about possible trauma from the birth. However, as Kayla began to demonstrate normal achievement of developmental milestones, such as rolling over, crawling, and walking, he became less concerned. Although her speech milestones did not seem to be coming along as well as her development in other areas, the pediatrician told Mr. and Mrs. McKenzie not to worry because Kayla's receptive language was well above average. He assumed that expressive language would follow on its own schedule of development. This assurance seemed to satisfy Mr. McKenzie, but not Mrs. McKenzie, who wanted to take Kayla to a specialist for an independent evaluation. Mr. McKenzie refused to have this done and accused Mrs. McKenzie of being neurotic, among other things. The couple fought bitterly over this point for a year and a half. During this time, Kayla's behavior became worse and worse. Since she could not make her needs known to her parents, she would become so frustrated that she would release her anger by throwing any nearby objects. Things eventually became so bad that little by little all breakables were put away so that Kayla would not throw them in a fit of anger. The family substituted plastic dishes for their stoneware and plastic tumblers for their glassware. Babysitters would come only once—the first time—and were never available thereafter. Although Mr. and Mrs. McKenzie did not acknowledge it, their home often resembled a war zone.

Finally, Mrs. McKenzie took Kayla to a child development clinic when she turned 4. She was diagnosed as having a severe speech impairment, and it was recommended that she begin therapy immediately. When Mr. McKenzie found out Mrs. McKenzie had taken his daughter for an evaluation in spite of his objection, he moved out of the family home. Kayla's behavior seemed to become even worse after this. Mrs. McKenzie's anxiety increased, and she began to have bouts of depression that depleted her energy. When her husband was in the house, she was able to try to manage Kayla's behavior, but with Mr. McKenzie gone, it was as if she just gave up. She knows that she is about to lose her job because of Kayla's problems at school, but she feels helpless to do anything about it.

Case Study Activity

INDIVIDUAL OR GROUP CASE ANALYSIS

Answer the following questions and be prepared to discuss them in class.

1. Whom should Mrs. Chung go to for help? Should she explain her situation to the principal? Should the speech therapist be giving her additional help? Whom else might she turn to?

_____

_____

_____

_____

_____

_____

_____

2. When a new teacher asks for help, is this request interpreted in a negative light by administrators? Why or why not?

_____

_____

_____

_____

_____

_____

_____

3. What is the relationship between Kayla's behavior and her speech impairment? Is sending Kayla home for throwing things a good strategy for managing this behavior? What other strategies might Mrs. Chung try?

_____

_____

_____

_____

_____

_____

_____

4. What has Kayla learned about misbehavior from her home environment? How might this situation have been different?

_____

_____

_____

_____

_____

_____

_____

_____

5. Does Kayla represent a danger to the other students in the classroom? Should she be in the regular classroom? Why or why not?

_____

_____

_____

_____

_____

_____

_____

6. If you were Mrs. Chung, would you attempt to provide any assistance to this family?

_____

_____

_____

_____

_____

_____

_____

_____

_____

7. Do you think that Kayla's behavior has anything to do with her parents' breakup? Why or why not? How is Mr. McKenzie's perspective different from Mrs. McKenzie's?

_____

_____

_____

_____

_____

_____

_____

_____

_____

_____

_____

Leroy

Leroy is a 9-year-old fourth grader at Bridgetown Elementary School. He is an average student with a pleasant personality. His teacher, Mrs. Masterson, is pleased with his work, but concerned about his speech. Leroy's voice has a very rough quality and an extremely low pitch. These unusual characteristics have earned him the nickname "Frogman." He is very popular with his peers so Mrs. Masterson isn't really worried about this teasing and Leroy seems to take it well, but she wonders if the way he talks is "normal." It appears to Mrs. Masterson that Leroy's voice deteriorates as the day progresses. Often during the last two periods of the day, his voice seems especially hoarse and has a strange, breathy quality.

During a recent parent-teacher conference, Mrs. Masterson mentioned Leroy's voice to his mother, Mrs. Hammond, and asked if he had always spoken in that manner. Mrs. Hammond chuckled and explained that Leroy's voice had been that way since he was born. She said that when he was a baby, Leroy was a real screamer and that nothing much had changed. Mrs. Hammond also explained that Leroy was very active in sports—soccer, baseball, and basketball—so he, his father, and four older brothers did a lot of loud cheering associated with this activity. She described their voices as "thundering through the house" when they were excited about a ballgame on television. Mrs. Hammond assured Mrs. Masterson that there was nothing wrong with Leroy's voice.

Mrs. Masterson continued to be concerned about this student. One day in the faculty lounge, she mentioned Leroy's unique vocal characteristics to two of his previous teachers. Both of these teachers smiled and said, "That's Leroy!" They told Mrs. Masterson that eventually she would get used to Leroy's voice and wouldn't even notice it as being unusual anymore.

Background Information:

Mrs. Masterson's brother was afflicted with laryngeal cancer in adulthood. His larynx was eventually removed, and he now uses an artificial larynx. Before the tumor was detected, her brother's voice quality was hoarse and raspy, not unlike that of Leroy's voice. Though this painful ordeal occurred a number of years ago, Mrs. Masterson is still very sensitive to vocal differences. Sometimes she wonders if she is too sensitive, thus calling attention to vocal differences that are characteristic of the normal range of functioning.

 Case Study Activity

INDIVIDUAL OR GROUP CASE ANALYSIS

Answer the following questions and be prepared to discuss them in class.

1. Should Mrs. Masterson refer Leroy for a speech–language evaluation? Why or why not? Why do you think that Leroy's previous teachers have not referred him for evaluation?

_____

_____

_____

_____

_____

_____

_____

2. Do Leroy's background and current hobbies tell you anything about his voice? What do you think may be causing his vocal problems? Do you think that other family members may have the same problem?

_____

_____

_____

_____

_____

_____

_____

_____

3. What type of modifications might be indicated for this student? What strategies could Mrs. Masterson implement in her classroom?

_____

_____

_____

_____

_____

_____

_____

4. What are the major characteristics of a voice disorder?

_____

_____

_____

_____

_____

_____

_____

5. Why is Leroy's voice quality different at the end of the day?

_____

_____

_____

_____

_____

_____

_____

6. If you were Mrs. Masterson, how could you explain to Mrs. Hammond that Leroy may need to be referred for a speech–language evaluation?

_____

_____

_____

_____

_____

_____

_____

_____

_____

_____

_____

_____

Mark

Mark is a 12-year-old sixth grader at Rushing East Middle School. Mrs. Clark, his English teacher, and Mrs. Orvieta, his Spanish teacher, have expressed concerns that this student seems to be extremely reticent and socially withdrawn in class. Mrs. Orvieta is especially concerned because so much of Mark's grade is dependent upon his class participation. Mark is never late for class and always scores high on the written Spanish exams, yet he just sits and shakes his head when she asks him to respond to her questions in Spanish. Mrs. Clark's concerns are somewhat similar. Mark's written work is excellent, but he refuses to answer questions in class. She reads his papers and feels that he is one of her best students, but he doesn't seem to know the answers to any questions she asks in class. She's starting to wonder if maybe his parents might be writing his papers for him. Both teachers have shared their thoughts with Mr. Exner, the school counselor.

When Mr. Exner interviewed Mark, he had the same thoughts that his teachers shared. Mark impressed him as an adolescent who didn't really have much to say and wasn't too concerned about his academic progress. The only rise Mr. Exner got out of him was when he suggested that Mark might drop Spanish and substitute a class that required less participation. Mark shook his head vehemently and said, "No." When Mr. Exner reviewed Mark's cumulative folder, he discovered that Mark had received services for speech from kindergarten through the fifth grade.

Mr. Exner decided to request Mark's special education file. When this file arrived, he found that Mark had been diagnosed with a severe fluency disorder in kindergarten and had received speech therapy for this problem until the fifth grade. At that time, the parents requested that the therapy be discontinued when Mark went on to middle school.

Background Information:

Mark's parents, Mr. and Mrs. Lupek, did not want speech therapy to be discontinued. Their son begged them to discontinue the service because he felt it would be too stigmatizing in middle school to be pulled out of class to work with the speech therapist. Mark also felt that he had made little progress with his stuttering in all those years of therapy. Mr. and Mrs. Lupek reluctantly agreed. Mark basically convinced them that he had gone as far as he could in speech and "the rest is up to me." He also convinced them that his time was better spent in content areas, and that he knew all the therapy strategies and could practice at home. As Mark is a very bright and mature adolescent, the Lupeks decided to let him make the decision regarding speech therapy in middle school.

As it turns out, Mark's only compensatory strategy for his fluency disorder has been to stop talking. He feels that at middle school he can "make it" with his written work, and he'll probably do better socially if he talks less.

Case Study Activity

INDIVIDUAL OR GROUP CASE ANALYSIS

Answer the following questions and be prepared to discuss them in class.

1. Should Mark be in speech therapy in middle school? Why or why not?

_____

_____

_____

_____

_____

_____

_____

2. Do you agree with the Lupeks' decision to let Mark decide what is best for himself because he is a "very bright and mature adolescent?" Why or why not?

_____

_____

_____

_____

_____

_____

_____

3. Is the curriculum so different in middle school as compared to elementary school that Mark could be successful by doing well with written work? Explain your response.

_____

_____

_____

_____

_____

_____

4. Why do you think Mark didn't mind speech therapy in elementary school, but now refuses this service in middle school? Give three reasons.

_____

_____

_____

_____

_____

_____

_____

5. Is it likely that Mark will eventually grow out of his stuttering problem? Why or why not?

_____

_____

_____

_____

_____

_____

_____

6. What can teachers do in the classroom to decrease the stress that stutterers feel when speaking and to discourage others from teasing the speaker? Give four strategies.

_____

_____

_____

_____

_____

_____

_____

7. Should Mark drop out of Spanish because of its oral participation requirement? If you were Mr. Exner, would you continue to try to counsel him out of these types of courses? Explain your answers.

_____

_____

_____

_____

_____

_____

_____

_____

_____

_____

_____

Richard

Richard is a 9-year-old student at Canyon Hills Elementary. He has recently moved to this town in Montana from Louisiana. Mr. Osage, Richard's third-grade teacher, has referred Richard for special education evaluation because of a speech problem. Mr. Osage estimates that anywhere from 50% to 75% of Richard's speech in unintelligible. Richard has been in the third grade for a month now, and things seem to be getting worse for this child. He does not appear to have any friends, and Mr. Osage attributes this to Richard's speech problem—his classmates cannot understand him either. Mr. Osage is disturbed that his third graders are making fun of Richard's speech. He has noticed that Richard is becoming more and more withdrawn, but he's not sure what to do about it. Mr. Osage has called the parents, Mr. and Mrs. Arceneau, in to discuss Richard's problem, only to discover that they have the same speech pattern as their son. Mr. Osage believes now that the problem must be of a genetic nature. He hopes that the pupil assessment team can identify Richard's problem, so that he can be placed in a class where he will receive the help he apparently needs. Mr. and Mrs. Arceneau seemed upset about the special education evaluation, saying that their son has not had school problems in the past.

Background Information:

Richard's cumulative folder from Louisiana indicates that he received all As and Bs on previous report cards. Teachers wrote only positive remarks about his behavior and academic progress. Mr. Osage is puzzled by the fact that he seems to be doing so poorly in his new school. He wonders if Richard is developing an emotional problem that is interfering with his school achievement. The speech therapist, Mrs. Gerkin, who has been practicing for 30 years, told Mr. Osage that she has never heard a speech pattern similar to that of Richard's. However, Mrs. Gerkin was born and raised in Montana, and she prides herself in telling others that there's no reason to leave the state because it's the most beautiful in the country. She is looking forward to completing her evaluation of Richard because she has never had a case such as this. She will probably recommend that Richard be staffed into a special education language delay class in a neighboring school district 25 miles away.

Case Study Activity

INDIVIDUAL OR GROUP CASE ANALYSIS

Answer the following questions and be prepared to discuss them in class.

1. With the information you have available, do you think there is another explanation for Richard's speech difference? Explain your answer.

_____

_____

_____

_____

_____

_____

_____

_____

_____

_____

2. What do you think of Mr. Osage's observation that Richard's speech problem is genetic because his parents share the same pattern of speech? What is another explanation?

_____

_____

_____

_____

_____

_____

_____

_____

_____

_____

_____

_____

_____

3. Why would Mrs. Gerkin want Richard to be staffed into a language delay class when his Louisiana reports indicate that his achievement is normal? Do you think that this is an appropriate placement for Richard?

_____

_____

_____

_____

_____

_____

_____

_____

_____

_____

_____

_____

4. Do you think that Richard's speech problem has anything to do with his behavior since he moved to Canyon Hills? Why or why not?

_____

_____

_____

_____

_____

_____

_____

_____

_____

_____

_____

5. Mr. Osage's position seems to be that it is normal for his third graders to make fun of Richard, and that there isn't anything he can do about it. If you were this teacher, describe three specific strategies you would use to socially integrate this student into your classroom.

_____

_____

_____

_____

_____

_____

_____

_____

_____

_____

_____

_____

6. Explain the distinction between language disorders and language differences. Should speech–language therapy be provided regardless of whether the variation is sociocultural or pathological in nature? Why or why not?

_____

_____

_____

_____

_____

_____

_____

_____

_____

_____

_____

_____

Seth

Seth is a 6-year-old student at Nichols Elementary School. He is a very bright little boy who has a mild articulation problem, mainly with the *r* and *th* sounds. His kindergarten teacher, Ms. Bellugi, is not really concerned about this difficulty because she has seen so many other children with the same problem. There are a couple of kindergartners who have made fun of Seth when he misarticulates certain words, such as his name, which he pronounces as *Sef*, but Ms. Bellugi has talked to those students and feels that she has controlled the matter. Ms. Bellugi feels that Seth is doing well in her class. She has noticed that he often plays by himself, but she has attributed this to his shy personality. She feels that as the school year progresses, he will become more comfortable and will start to make more friends.

Seth's parents, Mr. and Mrs. Kahn, are concerned about Seth's articulation. On the first day of school, they met with Ms. Bellugi and asked her to refer Seth for speech therapy. Although Ms. Bellugi did not really feel this was necessary, she agreed to complete the referral because of the parents' insistence. The speech therapist screened Seth and determined that his misarticulation was probably a normal aspect of his development. The therapist explained that Seth's speech difficulty did not constitute an educational problem, and thus therapy would not be warranted. She also mentioned that the school district would rescreen Seth as he developed to make sure that he was progressing normally as his age level advanced. The speech therapist told the parents that most children with articulation problems like Seth's learn to articulate all of their sounds by the age of 8. Mr. and Mrs. Kahn did not accept the therapist's recommendation. They told her that if speech therapy were not provided to their son within the next month, they would take legal action. They further indicated that their child's speech problem was causing him to have emotional problems, resulting in social isolation.

Background Information:

Mr. and Mrs. Kahn have two other children, both of whom were verbally precocious. Seth's siblings spoke in clear, lengthy sentences by the age of 2. They were also very extroverted children who made friends easily and were involved in numerous social activities from an early age. It is very disturbing to the parents that Seth's development seems to be lagging behind. They believe their son needs help, and they want to make sure he gets it. Mrs. Kahn's older sister is a speech–language therapist in private practice. She has encouraged the family to pursue services that she says, by law, should be provided to her nephew.

 Case Study Activity

INDIVIDUAL OR GROUP CASE ANALYSIS

Answer the following questions and be prepared to discuss them in class.

1. Should Seth receive speech therapy for his articulation problems? Do you think that his misarticulation constitutes an educational problem? Why or why not?

_____

_____

_____

_____

_____

_____

2. Do you think that Seth's speech difficulty is causing him to have social problems? Explain your response.

_____

_____

_____

_____

_____

_____

_____

3. Why is the school's perspective different from that of Mr. and Mrs. Kahn? Do you think that it makes sense to wait for Seth's articulation to develop, or do you believe it is better to take care of the problem before it escalates? Explain your response.

_____

_____

_____

_____

_____

_____

_____

_____

_____

4. What laws might influence this case? How could these laws be used by one or both parties?

_____

_____

_____

_____

_____

_____

_____

_____

5. How could the pupil assessment team and Ms. Bellugi work with this family to reach a compromise?

_____

_____

_____

_____

_____

_____

_____

_____

_____

_____

_____

_____

Yuri

Yuri is a 16-year-old student at Woodrow Wilson High School. Yuri and his family immigrated to the United States from Azerbaijan 2 years ago. Yuri was recently evaluated by the pupil assessment team. His IQ testing suggested that he was functioning in the mildly retarded range, with adaptive behavior skills falling in the borderline to low normal range. The pupil assessment team at Woodrow Wilson has recommended that Yuri be identified as mentally retarded so he can receive special education services in his regular education classes. Woodrow Wilson does not have any pull-out programs. The philosophy of the school is to provide additional help in the classroom to assist the student with the regular education objectives.

Yuri's parents do not speak English, but his uncle, who does, has come to the school meetings to listen to the recommendations and interpret them to Yuri's parents, Mr. and Mrs. Scrincosky. The family is adamantly opposed to the idea of having their son identified as being mentally retarded, but they recognize the fact that he needs help. The assessment team has told the family that Yuri doesn't qualify for special services under any other disability, so if he is going to get help, the parents will have to sign the papers that specify mental retardation as the disability condition.

Background Information:

When Yuri entered Woodrow Wilson 2 years ago, he did not speak any English. He was placed in the English as a Second Language (ESL) program. His ESL teacher, Mrs. Cuvo, was an energetic teacher who was firmly committed to the collaborative model of service delivery. She developed a program for Yuri that was based on close cooperation with his regular education teachers. Mrs. Cuvo kept a detailed notebook of Yuri's curriculum and assignments for each class so that she could assist him with the achievement of specific goals for each subject. Although Yuri's grades fell into the C to D range, Mrs. Cuvo felt that he was making significant progress considering his lack of familiarity with the English language.

After 2 years of receiving these educational services, Yuri took the conversational proficiency exam, which the district requires of all students. He passed the test and was immediately staffed out of the ESL program. Mrs. Cuvo did not want Yuri to leave the program, but it is the school district's policy to staff out all students who reach conversational proficiency on the ESL exam. Without Mrs. Cuvo's assistance, Yuri promptly began flunking all of his subjects. At this point, his regular education teachers, wanting to help him, referred him for special education evaluation.

Although the members of the assessment team are well aware of Yuri's language difficulties, they believe that his school problems are related to his limited potential as opposed to his lack of proficiency in English. This position is based on the premise that since Yuri has passed the ESL exam, he has achieved proficiency in the language. The speech–language therapist on the pupil assessment team is the only member who is not in agreement with this recommendation. However, she has decided to go along with the team's recommendation because she knows Yuri needs help, and this is the only way he is going to receive it. She doesn't think that the label of "mental retardation" should be considered an obstacle to getting services for this adolescent.

 ## Case Study Activity

INDIVIDUAL OR GROUP CASE ANALYSIS

Answer the following questions and be prepared to discuss them in class.

1. Does the diagnosis of mental retardation appear to be appropriate in Yuri's case? Why or why not?

_____

_____

_____

_____

_____

_____

_____

_____

2. What do adaptive behavior scales measure? What kinds of items might appear on these tests? Why do you think that Yuri's scores were so low on this test?

_____

_____

_____

_____

_____

_____

_____

_____

_____

_____

3. What is the purpose of a conversational proficiency exam? What is the relationship between conversational proficiency and academic achievement? Would it be possible to pass such an exam and still not have the language skills necessary for academic achievement? Why or why not?

_____

_____

_____

_____

_____

_____

_____

_____

_____

_____

4. What do you think that Mr. and Mrs. Scrincosky should do? Should they accept the special education services even though they do not agree with the label of mental retardation? What would you recommend in this situation?

_____

_____

_____

_____

_____

_____

_____

_____

_____

5. What type of educational plan would be the most appropriate for Yuri's instructional needs?

_____

_____

_____

_____

_____

_____

_____

_____

_____

Pervasive Developmental Needs

CHAPTER 7

Amber

Amber is a 7-year-old kindergarten student at Crossroads Elementary. She is repeating kindergarten because of socialization problems that were encountered last year. She has now been in kindergarten for 3 months, and her teacher, Mrs. Hsu, is concerned because Amber does not seem to be making any significant progress in this area. Amber does not have any friends, nor does she demonstrate an interest in socializing with her peers. She does not make eye contact with the children or the teacher, and she usually turns away from the person who is talking to her. She is also preoccupied with hair twirling. She will grab a lock of her hair, twirl it as tightly as possible, and then let it go, only to grab another lock and start the procedure over again. She engages in this behavior so frequently that a fairly large section of her hair is broken off about a half inch from the roots. This behavior is quite distracting to people who are trying to interact with her. Amber doesn't seem to have any of the typical interests of most kindergartners. For example, she has little interest in holidays or in the parties celebrating them. She was the only child who did not want to wear a costume for Halloween. When Mrs. Hsu tried to encourage her to join in, Amber asked her in a matter of fact way, "What for?"

Amber's only genuine interest seems to be in telephone directories, both the yellow and white pages. She has a strange fascination with reading the names and telephone numbers. She would rather do this than read any of the brightly colored picture books that are on display in the classroom. During show-and-tell Amber always brings in a section of the yellow pages. In great detail she will describe the companies listed under whatever section she is focusing on for that day. For example, one day the topic was heating repair companies. She read each name and address until Mrs. Hsu stopped her because the other children were getting

edgy. What is interesting to Mrs. Hsu is that Amber could go on for what seems like hours, talking about a topic in which most kindergartners have no interest. Mrs. Hsu has also found it interesting that Amber seems to have no interest in how these companies could be of service to an individual in everyday life. She just wants to read the listings.

In the 20 years that Mrs. Hsu has been teaching kindergarten, she has never seen a child such as Amber. In terms of readiness skills, most of Amber's work is above that of her peers. This is partly due to the fact that she has been retained, but even last year, Amber did not have problems with academics. Her letter and word recognition is well above the first-grade level. She has very strong skills in math, but she has problems with math papers because her writing is so poor. Much of Amber's writing is illegible, but Mrs. Hsu feels that this skill area will become stronger with practice and development. It is Amber's obvious lack of interest in socialization that is of greater concern to Mrs. Hsu. She is greatly troubled by the fact that she doesn't know how to help this child.

Background Information:

When Amber first started kindergarten, she was the only child in Mrs. Hsu's class who could read. Mrs. Hsu was so impressed with Amber's reading that she assumed the child was gifted. She sent her to the back of the room with a stack of advanced books while the other children were in their regular reading groups. One day Amber asked Mrs. Hsu if she could bring in the yellow pages to read during reading time. Mrs. Hsu was amused by this request and agreed. What Mrs. Hsu didn't realize was that Amber wanted to read from the phone book every day, which, of course, her teacher did not think was appropriate. Mrs. Hsu referred her for evaluation for the gifted and talented program. The coordinator sent back a report indicating that Amber scored in the low average range on all of the tests. Mrs. Hsu was somewhat embarrassed that she had misjudged this child to the extent that she had.

During a parent–teacher conference, Mrs. Hsu shared her concerns about Amber's socialization problems with her mother, Mrs. Stoner. Mrs. Stoner said she knew her daughter was different, but she felt that Amber was just developing according to her own schedule. When Amber did not make the desired social progress in kindergarten, Mrs. Stoner was not opposed to holding her back another year. However, she did have one request. Amber's mother wanted to be assured that Mrs. Hsu would be her teacher again. She insisted that Amber really admired Mrs. Hsu and had become very attached to her. Mrs. Stoner feared that Amber would regress if she were given another teacher and had to start all over building a relationship with a new teacher. Mrs. Hsu can hardly believe that Amber is attached to her, as this child had not made eye contact with her but half a dozen times in the course of the academic year. She reluctantly agreed to have her again, but she was not looking forward to the experience.

 Case Study Activity

INDIVIDUAL OR GROUP CASE ANALYSIS

Answer the following questions and be prepared to discuss them in class.

1. Should Amber be referred for a special education evaluation? Why or why not?

_____

_____

_____

_____

_____

_____

_____

_____

2. Based on the description in this case study, do you think that this child has a disability? If yes, what type of disability might this be?

_____

_____

_____

_____

_____

_____

_____

3. Should Mrs. Hsu be Amber's teacher again? Why or why not?

_____

_____

_____

_____

_____

_____

_____

4. Should Amber have been held back in kindergarten? Why or why not?

_____

_____

_____

_____

_____

_____

_____

_____

5. What types of strategies would you use to increase Amber's socialization? Describe four of these.

_____

_____

_____

_____

_____

_____

_____

6. What would you do about Amber's fascination with phone directories? Would you encourage, discourage, or ignore this interest? Explain your response.

_____

_____

_____

_____

_____

_____

_____

_____

_____

7. What kinds of strategies would you use to try to get Amber more interested in the kindergarten curriculum, for example, holiday celebrations and parties? Why do you think she has no interest in these topics?

_____

_____

_____

_____

_____

_____

_____

_____

_____

8. Explain how Amber's scores fell in the low average range when the gifted and talented coordinator tested her, yet she displays such high functioning in Mrs. Hsu's class.

_____

_____

_____

_____

_____

_____

_____

_____

Brenna

Brenna is a 6-year-old first-grade student at Westfall Elementary School. From the age of 3, she has been in a special education program for preschool students with disabilities. This is Brenna's first year in the mainstream. Her first-grade teacher, Mrs. Escammila, volunteered to have Brenna in her classroom, but she is starting to have second thoughts. Brenna's behavior has been quite disruptive to Mrs. Escammila's class. When Brenna becomes upset, she makes loud guttural sounds for long periods of time and beats her fist on the desk. Sometimes, when she's very upset, she falls to the floor and rolls around while making the loud noises. These incidents last anywhere from 30 to 45 minutes and appear to be precipitated by noises in the classroom environment. For example, the pencil sharpener always causes a problem. A siren down the street, children walking by the classroom, a film being shown to a neighboring class, or any announcement over the public address system can potentially cause Brenna to experience stress. Although Brenna has a full-time aide assigned to her, the aide is not able to calm her enough to stop the outburst.

Mrs. Escammila believes in inclusion, but she is starting to question whether this is the most suitable learning environment for Brenna. She is also concerned about her other students. She can tell they are frustrated by their classroom situation. Whenever Brenna has an outburst, the class basically has to stop all oral activities because of the noise level of the outburst. Mrs. Escammila has gently broached the subject of placing Brenna into a special education classroom with Brenna's mother, Mrs. Lohrman, but with little success. Mrs. Lohrman felt that the 3 years Brenna spent in a noncategorical preschool special education program were more negative than positive because of the behaviors exhibited by her classmates. Mrs. Escammila doesn't know what to do now.

Background Information:

At the age of 2, Mrs. Lohrman brought Brenna to the local university's developmental disabilities clinic for a complete evaluation. At that time, Brenna had little expressive language, numerous behavioral peculiarities, and limited social skills. The evaluation team felt that although Brenna displayed many autistic-like behaviors, such as self-stimulation, insistence on sameness, and poor interaction with the environment, she also displayed a pattern of high functioning on adaptive behavior measures and tests of visual–motor problem solving. They finally diagnosed her as being severely language impaired and recommended the special education preschool program for her. Mrs. Lohrman was hopeful that this program would give Brenna the communication and socialization skills necessary to begin first grade in a regular classroom. However, this program did not turn out to be ideal.

The preschool special education class served a population of children who were multiply disabled, and Brenna did not get the peer interaction that Mrs. Lohrman was hoping she would. Three of Brenna's classmates were autistic; three were severely mentally retarded with cerebral palsy; two were deaf and blind; and one child was nonverbal, nonambulatory, and profoundly retarded. In short, there was very little language stimulation in that classroom other than what was being provided by the specialists. Brenna's communication skills improved only slightly and, according to Mrs. Lohrman's perception, her behavior worsened. When she entered the program, her behaviors were mainly hand flapping and spinning. By the time she was staffed out of the program, she had added finger flicking and head slapping, much to her mother's dismay. After considerable thought, Mrs. Lohrman decided that Brenna would never again be subjected to a situation in which she would regress due to the atypical behavior exhibited by other children. She has experienced a lot of guilt for allowing her daughter to stay in that classroom for 3 years.

Case Study Activity

INDIVIDUAL OR GROUP CASE ANALYSIS

Answer the following questions and be prepared to discuss them in class.

1. What kinds of strategies might Mrs. Escammila try to decrease Brenna's behavioral outbursts? Give four examples.

_____

_____

_____

_____

_____

_____

_____

2. What other resources might Mrs. Escammila use to solve this problem with Brenna's behavior?

_____

_____

_____

_____

_____

_____

_____

3. Was Brenna's special education preschool class appropriate for her needs? Why or why not?

_____

_____

_____

_____

_____

_____

_____

4. If you were the parent of one of Brenna's classmates in Mrs. Escammila's class, would you take any action in this situation? Why or why not?

_____

_____

_____

_____

_____

_____

_____

5. Does Brenna have a legal right to be in that first-grade classroom? Support your answer.

_____

_____

_____

_____

_____

_____

_____

6. Do you agree with Mrs. Lohrman's perspective in regard to Brenna's placement in regular education? Why or why not?

_____

_____

_____

_____

_____

_____

_____

7. If you were Brenna's teacher, explain how you might work with this parent to increase this child's opportunity for success in the first grade.

_____

_____

_____

_____

_____

_____

Greg

Greg is a 13-year-old seventh grader at Medford Middle School. He is currently failing three subjects and receiving Cs and Ds in the others. His mother, Mrs. Wiecinsky, is desperately trying to get him some help, but so far her requests have not been well received by Greg's teachers. Greg has been identified as having Asperger's syndrome by a psychiatrist in an independent evaluation. The psychiatrist's report stated that Greg would require some significant modifications in the school environment to help him achieve commensurate with his ability level. One of these modifications was that Greg's teachers should go over his assignments with him after class so that he understands what he is to do. Another recommended modification specified that each teacher should ask him if he needs help when he is completing seatwork or taking an exam in class. Mrs. Wiecinsky has not been able to convince one teacher that Greg genuinely needs this assistance to be successful. Of the three courses that Greg is currently failing—history, English, and sociology—none of the teachers are willing to make any changes whatsoever. These teachers seem to think that Greg is lazy and slow. Since Greg has not been identified as a student with special education needs, the teachers have taken the position that he should conform to the same expectations they hold for the rest of the class. One of these teachers has also told Mrs. Wiecinsky that she doesn't believe there is such a thing as Asperger's syndrome, and that it sounds like an excuse for her son's failure to conform to school requirements.

When Mrs. Wiecinsky went to the principal to ask for help, he referred her to his assistant principal, who referred her to the guidance counselor, who gave her a list of local mental health professionals who might be able to counsel her son. Mrs. Wiecinsky feels like she is at the end of her rope. She fears Greg will end up failing most of his subjects as he did last year. She doesn't know where to go or whom to turn to.

Background Information:

Greg has always been an unusual child in that he displayed a number of strengths in marked contrast to his weaknesses. For example, at the age of 6, he had memorized all the commuter train stops for the city of Chicago from a Chicago Transit Authority map that his aunt had inadvertently left at his home after taking a business trip to that city. Greg had never been to Chicago, nor was the family planning a trip to that destination. The city is 2,000 miles from his hometown, and he does not know anyone who lives there. In spite of the fact that this city did not seem to have any connection with his life, Greg began to display a great degree of enthusiasm in learning and reciting this information. Whenever Greg's mother would have company, Greg would immediately launch into a description of the different train lines, the specific stops, and the time between each stop. His extraordinary ability to memorize this information stood in marked contrast to his inability to memorize and use the simplest of polite conventions. He could never remember to say hello or good-bye to visitors. He never said thank you to anyone bringing him gifts. When his mother chided him about this, he always said, "I forget what to say." As far back as Mrs. Wiecinsky could remember, Greg has never had a friend. He has never been asked over to a child's home, with the exception of a couple of birthday parties to which his whole class had been invited.

Greg was able to be a fairly successful student throughout elementary school. His strengths in single word reading, math computations, and spelling (he won the school spelling bee every year for 6 years) were so great that teachers often overlooked his weaknesses in comprehension and problem solving. All of his teachers found him to be an unusual child because of his poor social skills and his continued interest in the Chicago Transit Authority commuter train lines.

When he started middle school, Greg immediately began having major school problems. His ability to answer true/false, fill-in-the-blank, and multiple-choice questions in elementary school did not prepare him for the essay question exams and expository assign-ments characteristic of the middle school curriculum. At the end of the first reporting period, he was failing all subjects with the exception of math. His teachers identified the problem as a lack of motivation. Mrs. Wiecinsky initiated a parent referral and requested a full special education evaluation. Although the school did not think that this was necessary, they agreed to do the evaluation because Mrs. Wiecinsky demanded it. The results indicated that Greg's IQ was 95. Single word reading was at the 10th-grade level, math computations were at the 9th-grade level, and spelling was above the 12th-grade level; however, math reasoning was found to be at the 4th-grade level and reading comprehension was at the 5th-grade level. The assessment team did not find evidence of any learning problem that met the criteria for a disability condition. They told Mrs. Wiecinsky that Greg's social problems were unrelated to his school progress. They inferred that Greg's lack of motivation could be attributed to his parents' divorce 10 years prior and recommended that she get him a counselor to help him deal with this problem.

 ## Case Study Activity

INDIVIDUAL OR GROUP CASE ANALYSIS

Answer the following questions and be prepared to discuss them in class.

1. Describe Asperger's syndrome. Explain the specific characteristics of this disability and discuss how they are related to Greg's characteristics.

_____

_____

_____

_____

_____

_____

_____

2. Explain how it is possible for the psychiatrist's report to specify a disability condition, and yet the special education evaluation at the school did not uncover one.

_____

_____

_____

_____

_____

_____

_____

_____

_____

3. Why do you think that Greg's teachers are refusing to provide him the assistance recommended in the psychiatrist's report?

_____

_____

_____

_____

_____

_____

_____

_____

4. Does Mrs. Wiecinsky have any legal recourse if Greg's teachers continue to refuse to provide him with these modifications? Explain the different options that might be available to her.

_____

_____

_____

_____

_____

_____

_____

_____

5. If you were asked to be an advocate for this family, explain how you would help resolve this problem.

_____

_____

_____

_____

_____

_____

_____

_____

Paul

Paul is a 16-year-old student at Middleton High School. He attends a program for adolescents with severe disabilities for most of the instructional day. He is mainstreamed for physical education and lunch. Paul is an autistic student with severe communication and socialization problems. Although he is verbal, the only way he can use language is to echo back what he has heard in his environment. He apparently has no formulation ability of his own. Facilitated communication has been tried with Paul, but without any success. He has been successful in learning approximately six signs, and he has a language board with pictures of 10 other events or requests that he sometimes uses.

Paul's social problems are of concern to both his teachers and his mother, Mrs. Wender. When Paul becomes frustrated, he physically strikes out at those in his environment. Sometimes he resorts to biting instead of hitting. Paul's special education teacher, Mr. Hirsch, believes that Paul is using physical aggression because of his frustration with communication. Many times he becomes so frustrated and upset that he forgets to use the communication system to which he has access. This has been a long-standing problem with Paul, but it has worsened as his size has increased. When he was young and small, his teachers and mother could more easily handle his outbursts. Now that he is almost 5'10" and 200 pounds, his behavior has become more difficult to manage. Paul

has a full-time aide, Mr. Jackson, whose sole responsibility is to assist Paul with his communication and socialization. Oftentimes, this means that Mr. Jackson has to physically restrain him from hitting another student in the classroom, in the physical education class, or in the hall.

In the classroom, Paul becomes easily upset if another student changes something in the environment, such as pulling the blinds down, moving a table around the room, or listening to an audio tape without using the headphones. Paul is very sensitive to these changes and appears to need a great deal of structure and sameness in his environment. Mr. Hirsch and Mr. Jackson have decided that the best way to work with Paul is to have a corner of the classroom designated as his space. They have structured the classroom in a way that provides Paul with an eight-by-eight-foot section that is surrounded by three-foot bookshelves on two sides and two adjoining walls on the other two sides. Mr. Jackson stays with Paul in this section and provides him one-to-one communication instruction. When Paul is having a good day, Mr. Jackson brings him out to interact with the other students in the classroom for as long as Paul can tolerate the interaction.

Although neither Mr. Hirsch nor Mr. Jackson would describe this program as being optimal, they both felt it was working pretty well considering the circumstances of Paul's behavior. Unfortunately two incidents occurred yesterday that are causing them to rethink Paul's placement. During swimming, Paul attacked another student who dove in the pool in front of him in an attempt to swim over to his own class. It was clear that the student scared Paul, who reacted by grabbing his arm and refusing to let go. It took Mr. Jackson and two other teachers to pry Paul's hands off the student. Needless to say, the other student was pretty shaken up. Then at lunch, another student came up behind Paul and gave him a pat on the back, taking Paul by surprise. Paul reacted by throwing his whole tray at the student and again had to be restrained by several adults. The student who had greeted Paul was angry and embarrassed.

As a result of these attacks, the principal, Mrs. Yates, now has two complaints from angry parents. She has asked the pupil assessment team to review Paul's placement. Her feeling is that he needs to be in a more restrictive placement, such as a special school that serves students with severe behavioral needs. Mrs. Wender is upset because she is afraid that the school has given up on Paul. Her greatest fear is that he will be sent to a residential facility where he will be physically restrained and mistreated.

Background Information:

From the first year of life, it was clear to Paul's parents that he was different from other children. He cried about 6 hours a day, sometimes more, from 2 months of age to almost 2 years of age. His cries were such that his parents felt he was in terrible pain. They took him from doctor to doctor trying to uncover the source of his discomfort. When Paul was 20 months old, one of these doctors told the parents that they would just have to learn to live with the crying because there was no physical cause that could be treated. The next day, Mr. Wender left. He filed for a divorce shortly thereafter. He has had no contact with his son since that time.

Mrs. Wender continued to seek out help from the medical community. Around the age of 2 years, Paul's crying diminished somewhat. This brought his mother some relief, but then she began to be distressed by other behaviors he started demonstrating. For example, he stopped making eye contact with anyone, including her. It was as if Paul looked through people as opposed to looking at them. He began insisting that everything in his room and most of the house be situated in the same way he left it. If he lined up two dozen dominoes on the living room floor, he wanted them left in that position. Mrs. Wender soon found that it was easier to leave things the way Paul wanted them rather than face the extreme behavioral outbursts that resulted from moving his things. By the time Paul was 2 years old, he had been diagnosed as severely autistic.

Mrs. Wender's life has revolved around her son and his needs. Her friends have accused her of being a martyr for Paul. They believe that he should have been institutionalized many years ago, so that she could have some life of her own. Mrs. Wender has been involved in parent support groups for families with autistic children for many years. She has heard nightmarish stories of children who were institutionalized and ended up either in a drugged stupor or in physical restraints in facilities that were understaffed and unable to meet the needs of any child, let alone one with needs like Paul's. She knows that Paul's behavior and his size make him a candidate for such a placement. She is also uncertain about how much longer she can control his behavior in her own home. Mrs. Wender lives in fear that one of his outbursts will result in him throwing a chair through the living room window or something worse. She knows Paul will never be able to live in a group home situation, not unless his behavior changes drastically. Her only hope is that Middleton High School will continue to keep him and provide him with the full-time aide that allows him to be included to some degree.

 ## Case Study Activities

PART I:
INDIVIDUAL CASE ANALYSIS

To complete this part, write two letters to be considered in this placement review. In the first letter, assume the role of Mrs. Wender and write a letter to the pupil assessment team, stating why you believe Paul's current placement at Middleton is the most appropriate for his needs. In the second letter, assume the role of Mrs. Yates and ask the pupil assessment team to consider removing Paul from Middleton to a more restrictive setting.

PART II:
INDIVIDUAL OR GROUP CASE ANALYSIS

Answer the following questions and be prepared to discuss them in class.

1. Do you consider Paul's current educational placement and circumstances to be inclusive? Why or why not?

_____

_____

_____

_____

_____

_____

2. Do you think that Paul should be excluded from physical education? Should Paul have his lunch in the special education classroom instead of the school lunchroom? Explain your answers.

_____

_____

_____

_____

_____

_____

3. If you were Mrs. Yates, how would you handle parent complaints regarding the two recent incidents of Paul's aggressive behavior?

_____

_____

_____

_____

_____

_____

4. Should Paul be placed in a more restrictive environment? Why or why not?

_____

_____

_____

_____

_____

_____

_____

5. Can you think of any strategies that could diminish Paul's aggressive behavior?

_____

_____

_____

_____

_____

_____

_____

6. In your opinion, is the use of a full-time aide justified for this one student? Explain your position.

_____

_____

_____

_____

_____

_____

7. Do you think that Mrs. Wender has been given adequate support to help her raise this child in the past? Can you think of any ways that Mrs. Wender could be supported in her efforts to keep her son in her home and the community?

_____

_____

_____

_____

_____

_____

_____

8. What is the prognosis for Paul?

_____

_____

_____

_____

_____

_____

_____

Veru

Veru is a 10-year-old child at Waltonville Elementary School. He was diagnosed as autistic at the age of 3. Veru has been in a full-time special education class since he started school. This year he is to be included in a regular fifth-grade classroom for half of the instructional day. He will have an aide for most of this time, except for 1 hour of math. During this time, Mr. Wang, his fifth-grade teacher, will not have any assistance. Mr. Wang is reluctant to have Veru in the classroom because of the distracting behaviors he displays. One of the most disturbing behaviors is that of head banging. Veru has built up a huge mass of scar tissue on his forehead from banging his head against all sorts of surfaces. Veru's parents, Mr. and Mrs. Kishore, have made it clear that they consider it the teacher's responsibility to keep Veru from engaging in this self-injurious behavior. Other behaviors that Veru demonstrates are head and face slapping, biting, and hand flapping. He also makes loud groaning noises that are very upsetting to Mr. Wang.

Mr. and Mrs. Kishore believe it is in Veru's best interests to be mainstreamed as much as possible. It is their opinion that Veru has much more potential than

he has been credited as having. They are especially interested in having the school personnel use facilitated communication to encourage his language development. Veru's aide has been trained in the use of facilitated communication. She has been working closely with him for several months now, but she has not had much success with this method of communication. Regardless of the limited progress, Mr. and Mrs. Kishore have requested that the keyboard be used throughout the day. Their expectation is that Mr. Wang will also use it during math class when Veru's aide is not available. They have suggested to him that he could benefit from the facilitated communication training class that is sponsored by a local university. They have also suggested that Mr. Wang take a sign language class, as Veru uses about 20 basic signs, and they are hoping to see more growth in that area of communication. Mr. Wang cannot imagine undertaking a special course of training on his own time to benefit only one student in his class. As politely as possible, he has declined.

Mr. Wang has told the principal, Mr. Bridges, that he would really prefer that Veru be placed in one of the other fifth-grade classes with a teacher who perhaps has more experience and patience dealing with children like Veru. Mr. Bridges replied that since Mr. Wang is the only male teacher in the fifth grade and he has the most disciplined classroom in the building, he is the obvious choice to deal with behavioral problem children. The principal also reminded Mr. Wang that the Kishores are close friends of the superintendent. He has suggested that a conference be held with the Kishores to talk about their expectations for this school year.

Background Information:

Mr. and Mrs. Kishore are both highly educated professionals. Mr. Kishore has a PhD in physics and works with NASA, while Mrs. Kishore is a medical doctor and a research oncologist. Both parents were in their mid-forties when Veru was born. Although Veru displayed very slow development and atypical social behaviors from the first year of life, the Kishores were reluctant to accept the notion that something could be wrong. One of his preschool teachers referred him to Child Find because the parents did not agree with the teacher's recommendation that they seek a developmental evaluation for Veru. The Kishores finally did agree to the evaluation. However, they did not agree with the findings, which suggested that Veru's IQ fell into the moderate to severe range of mental retardation. It has always been their feeling that Veru's severe language disorder has prevented him from demonstrating his full potential. They are very excited about the possibility that facilitated communication may provide their son with the means of communication which has eluded him thus far.

The Kishores always felt it was a mistake to place Veru with other children who were autistic and retarded. They don't understand how he could possibly be challenged in that kind of an environment. Although they have tremendous respect for Mrs. Delgado, Veru's special education teacher, they really feel that Veru belongs in the mainstream with other children. Mrs. Delgado serves as the secretary for the local chapter of the National Autism Society, so she and the Kishores often find themselves working together for this organization. Mrs. Delgado is not sure that she agrees with the idea of including this student in the mainstream for half of the instructional day, but she's willing to provide as much support as she can to Veru and his family.

 Case Study Activities

PART I:
ROLE PLAYING

Break into groups of four or five. Assume one of the following roles: Mrs. Kishore, Mrs. Delgado, Mr. Wang, Mr. Bridges, and Mr. Kishore (an optional role). Simulate an IEP conference, the objective of which is to talk about expectations for Veru in Mr. Wang's fifth-grade class and to develop IEP goals. Use the IEP form included on page 190 to develop the IEP goals, and provide a summary of the conference in the space provided.

Conference Summary

_____

_____

_____

_____

_____

_____

_____

_____

_____

_____

_____

_____

_____

PART II:
INDIVIDUAL OR GROUP CASE ANALYSIS

Answer the following questions and be prepared to discuss them in class.

1. Should Veru be in a regular fifth-grade class for half of the instructional day? Why or why not?

_____

_____

_____

_____

_____

_____

_____

_____

_____

2. How can Mr. Wang modify his fifth-grade math class to accommodate Veru's needs?

_____

_____

_____

_____

_____

_____

_____

_____

3. What should Mr. Wang do to decrease Veru's head banging? How can he manage this behavior while he is teaching math class?

_____

_____

_____

_____

_____

_____

_____

_____

4. Should Mr. Wang be responsible for using facilitated communication during math class? Why or why not?

_____

_____

_____

_____

_____

_____

_____

_____

5. If you were Mr. Wang, would you try to learn sign language and facilitated communication in the training courses suggested by the parents? Why or why not? Do you think that this family expects too much from the regular classroom teacher?

_____

_____

_____

_____

_____

_____

_____

6. Do you agree with Mr. Bridges' idea that Mr. Wang should have Veru in his classroom because he is the only male teacher at Waltonville and a strong disciplinarian? How should these decisions be made by the school administration?

_____

_____

_____

_____

_____

_____

7. Do you think that the Kishores are realistic about their son's disability? Why or why not? Do you think that most parents are realistic about their children's strengths and weaknesses? Why do you think that teachers are often reluctant to accept the idea that parents may know as much or more about their children as professionals do?

_____

_____

_____

_____

_____

_____

8. How can the teachers in this school work with this family to maximize Veru's success in school? Give four strategies.

_____

_____

_____

_____

_____

School District #1
Individualized Educational Program

Student: _____

Current Functioning	Long-Term Goals	Short-Term Objectives

Sensory Needs

CHAPTER 8

Emilio

Emilio is a 9-year-old third grader at Mountain View Elementary. He has a bilateral mixed hearing loss that falls into the moderate to severe range. Emilio's hearing loss is thought to be related to a bout of meningitis, which occurred at the age of 13 months, and to frequent episodes of otitis media during the preschool years. His parents, Mr. and Mrs. Salinas, are not deaf. Emilio has four school-age siblings, all of whom are hearing. This will be Emilio's first year at Mountain View. His family has moved from a large city to this rural setting in the mountains. When Emilio lived in the city, he attended a center school for children with hearing impairments. The approach used by this school was total communication, which meant that Emilio was taught American Sign Language (ASL) in addition to his speech and language therapy. Mr. and Mrs. Salinas were dissatisfied with Emilio's previous school program. They have decided that they do not want their son to continue to learn ASL. They feel that it isolates Emilio from their family. At one time, the family made an effort to learn ASL, but after a brief period, they discovered how difficult it was and gave up.

Mr. Issacs, the principal of Mountain View Elementary, has been very welcoming to Emilio and his family. He explained to the family that his school did not have a hearing impairment program, but he felt that they could meet Emilio's educational needs. There is such a program at the neighboring school, which is 30 miles down the road. Mr. and Mrs. Salinas were told that if they chose that school, bus service would be provided to Emilio. The family declined, saying that they wanted Emilio to be in his neighborhood school with his siblings. Although Mr. Issacs does not have much experience with serving the needs of children with hearing impairments, he is eager to work with this child and his family. Mountain View has a special education resource teacher, Mrs.

Cartwright, who works with the other teachers to provide modifications for students with disabilities. Mr. Issacs feels confident that Mrs. Cartwright will be able to provide Emilio with the educational adaptations he needs to experience success.

Mr. and Mrs. Salinas met with Mr. Issacs and Mrs. Cartwright to discuss some of their concerns before the scheduled IEP meeting. Emilio's achievement test scores reveal that his reading and written expression are on a mid first-grade level, while his math is at approximately the late second-grade level. Computations have been identified as a strength, and problem solving has been identified as a weakness. Mr. and Mrs. Salinas are also concerned with Emilio's socialization. Although he had several good friends in the hearing impaired program at his previous school, he has never had a hearing friend. This is very upsetting to the family. Additionally, the parents referred to the problem of Emilio turning off his hearing aid. He has complained to his family that the hearing aid is uncomfortable and makes a disturbing sound, but his family has had it checked and rechecked. Emilio's doctors and his audiologist have strongly suggested that Emilio keep this aid on, because it is their feeling that it will maximize his residual hearing and help him in the classroom. As Emilio's speech is difficult to comprehend, speech therapy is a service that the family wants to continue along with speech reading. Neither of the parents wants Emilio to continue learning sign language. They want to shift from a total communication approach to an oralist approach.

Background Information:

Emilio's parents and grandparents were born in Mexico. Since Emilio's maternal grandparents live with the Salinas, Spanish is frequently spoken in the home environment. Mr. and Mrs. Salinas want their children to be fluent in the language of their native country, but they are also concerned that their children have good English language skills because they see this as a prerequisite to success in the United States. They are worried that Emilio will not be skilled in either language.

When Emilio's hearing impairment was identified at the age of 3, his parents had no understanding of the different types of problems he might encounter. They enrolled him in a preschool classroom that was part of a special education school for children with disabilities. Mr. and Mrs. Salinas did not like this school experience. Many of the children who attended this school had severe disabilities and were limited in their physical mobility and communication. However, they did not realize that they might have another choice for their son. After 2 years in this deaf preschool, Emilio was moved into a school that was closer to his neighborhood. This school was considered to be the center school for children with significant hearing impairments. The principal and the teacher both described Emilio's new program as being inclusive, providing him with many opportunities to socialize with the other children in the school. But as far as Mr. and Mrs. Salinas could see, this socialization never happened for Emilio or any of the other hearing impaired children. The program continued to provide a total communication education, as Emilio's preschool did. The elementary school also had a sign language program that taught ASL to the children without disabilities. But something seemed to be missing. Whenever Mrs. Salinas visited the school to have lunch with Emilio or to assist with playground duty, she always observed the same thing: the deaf children would play together on the playground and sit together in the lunchroom. She never saw Emilio or any of the other deaf students interact with the hearing students. When she discussed these concerns with the teacher of the program, she was told that Emilio did socialize with the hearing students and that integration was not a problem in that school. In the 2 years that Emilio was there, he was never invited over to a hearing child's home, and Mrs. Salinas never heard him refer to any friends other than those in the special education program.

 ## Case Study Activities

PART I:
ROLE PLAYING

Break into groups of four or five. The following roles should be assumed by group members: Mr. Salinas, Mrs. Cartwright, Mrs. Simons (Emilio's third-grade teacher), Mr. Issacs, and Mrs. Salinas (an optional role). Simulate an IEP meeting in which Emilio's educational needs are addressed. During this meeting the group should be sure to: (a) review current functioning, (b) identify strengths and weaknesses, (c) develop short and long term goals, (d) describe possible teaching strategies that will be used to achieve these goals, (e) explain the services to be provided, and (f) determine responsibility with regard to carrying out the educational plan. Use the IEP form included on page 195 to record the IEP goals.

PART II:
INDIVIDUAL OR GROUP CASE ANALYSIS

Answer the following questions and be prepared to discuss them in class.

1. What is a bilateral mixed hearing loss?

_____

_____

_____

_____

2. Do you think that Emilio should discontinue ASL instruction? Why or why not? Why do you think that Emilio's family is so opposed to this instruction?

_____

_____

_____

_____

_____

_____

_____

_____

3. If you were Emilio's third-grade teacher at Mountain View, what general strategies would you implement to encourage this student's success in the classroom?

_____

_____

_____

_____

_____

_____

_____

_____

4. Why do you think that Emilio did not experience much socialization with students without disabilities at his previous school? How can his new school help him to achieve more success in this area? Give four specific strategies for increasing socialization.

_____

_____

_____

_____

_____

_____

_____

_____

_____

5. Why do you think that Emilio is reading below grade level? Describe how you would approach reading instruction with this student. Give four specific strategies that you would use.

_____

_____

_____

_____

_____

_____

6. Do you think that the language background of Emilio's family will influence his acquisition of the English language? Explain your response.

_____

_____

_____

_____

_____

_____

Jake

Jake is a 14-year-old freshman at Walker High School. He has been profoundly deaf since shortly after birth as a result of cytomegalovirus. Jake is able to use his voice for communication only on a limited basis, as it is difficult for others to understand him. He has the benefit of an interpreter for algebra, English, and biology classes. Jake is an excellent speech reader who has been doing fairly well since he started at Walker High this fall. His first report card indicated that he was progressing in a satisfactory manner. He received mostly Cs with a B+ in biology. His parents, Mr. and Mrs. Penrod, are pleased with the way things are going.

Although Jake's teachers are not concerned about his academic progress, they are somewhat concerned about his emotional state. He always seems withdrawn, and he doesn't appear to have any friends. Mr. Keefe,

School District #1
Individualized Educational Program

Student: _____

Current Functioning	Long-Term Goals	Short-Term Objectives

who does quite a bit of cooperative learning in his social studies class, has noticed that Jake rarely participates in these group activities. Mrs. Kuhn, Jake's biology teacher, has observed that Jake doesn't seem interested in working with his lab partner. In fact, Jake's lab partner has complained to Mrs. Kuhn and has asked to be assigned to another partner. Apparently Jake does all of the work and then expects his partner to copy the answers from him. He doesn't show any interest in cooperative problem solving.

Background Information:

Jake started preschool at the age of 3 in a special education program for children with hearing impairments. Following this preschool experience, he attended a self-contained special education program in an elementary school that had a center for hearing impaired students. He stayed in this program for 6 years. When he was ready to go on to middle school, his parents asked that he be mainstreamed. The school district supported this placement because they were in the process of moving toward inclusion for all special education students. They also agreed to hire a half-time interpreter for Jake to assist in this transition.

During the 3 years that Jake spent in middle school, he began to demonstrate behavioral problems. He started skipping school and was apprehended for shoplifting. He also started showing signs of withdrawal and depression. The students who had been his peers during the elementary school years had either been transferred to other neighborhood middle schools or to the state school for students with visual and hearing impairments, which is 100 miles away. Jake's parents took him to see a psychologist, who diagnosed him as having an adjustment reaction. He recommended therapy, but Jake refused to go. It was at this time that Jake first brought up the idea of transferring to the state residential school. Mr. and Mrs. Penrod were surprised and dismayed at this idea. They are against the notion that deaf students can be better educated in a segregated setting. They are firmly committed to the idea that all people need to learn to live together in an integrated community. They are not interested in having their son spend more time communicating with sign language. They know that the state school uses the American Sign Language (ASL) approach to education, and they believe that Jake should spend more time attempting to use his speech for communication purposes. Jake's parents worry that he would be tempted to give up on using speech altogether if he were given that option.

Jake's interpreter, Mrs. Lucero, supports the idea of the transfer to the state school. She has commented several times that Jake appears to be lonely at Walker High School. She feels that he has decided he just doesn't fit in with the other adolescents in the mainstream. Mrs. Lucero's parents and two siblings are deaf, so she has a different perspective of Jake's situation. On one occasion she mentioned that Jake was missing out on the "experience of the deaf culture," and that could help him have more insight regarding the choices available to him.

 ## Case Study Activity

INDIVIDUAL OR GROUP CASE ANALYSIS

Answer the following questions and be prepared to discuss them in class.

1. If you were Jake's social studies teacher, how would you encourage his participation in cooperative learning activities for that class?

_____

_____

_____

_____

_____

_____

_____

_____

2. What would you do about Jake's lab partner if you were the biology teacher?

_____

_____

_____

_____

_____

_____

3. How would you know if Jake were experiencing normal adolescent problems or something more severe? Should his parents force him to see a psychologist? From a psychological perspective, what is an adjustment disorder?

_____

_____

_____

_____

_____

_____

4. What is Mrs. Lucero referring to when she says that Jake is missing out on the "deaf culture"? Why might she think that segregated education is preferable to his current integrated education?

_____

_____

_____

_____

_____

_____

_____

5. Why does Jake want to go to the school for students with hearing impairments? Could this be described as an expression of adolescent independence? Why or why not?

_____

_____

_____

_____

_____

_____

_____

6. Why does it seem so important for the Penrods to keep Jake at Walker High School? Give four possible reasons.

_____

_____

_____

_____

_____

_____

_____

7. Where do you think Jake should go to school? Why?

_____

_____

_____

_____

_____

_____

_____

Karen

Karen is a 17-year-old senior at Cannonville High School. She has retinitis pigmentosa, a genetic eye disease that progressively leads to blindness. Karen had been using large print books for the past 3 years, but the visual impairment has recently worsened to the extent that it is no longer possible for her to read print of any size. Ms. Ziebert, the special education resource teacher at Cannonville High, has been providing Karen with adapted materials since Karen started school there. Ms. Ziebert has also been in charge of collaborating with Karen's other teachers to ensure her success. However, there has actually been very little collaboration because Karen has been able to do everything that her peers have with few exceptions. This year will be different. Karen's parents, Mr. and Mrs. James, have informed Ms. Ziebert that a recent eye exam determined that Karen's vision had degenerated to 20/400 in her right eye and 20/450 in her left eye. The ophthalmologist has predicted that Karen's residual vision will be minimal by the end of this year. He has recommended that Karen learn Braille.

Karen flatly refuses to have anything to do with Braille. She wants to continue to go to her classes and learn as well as she can without any intervention. She feels that she can keep up with her studies by concentrating harder on the auditory aspects of instruction. Karen is struggling to keep her life as normal as possible. She wants to continue to be a member of the cheerleading squad, even though her parents want her to quit. It is very important for her to keep up with her friends. She and her boyfriend recently broke up—it was the boyfriend who initiated the split, and Karen suspects it had something to do with her failing eyesight. Karen has told both her parents and Ms. Ziebert that she is not going to have anything to do with mobility training. She indicated that she would rather spend the time studying for her driver's license exam.

Background Information:

Mr. and Mrs. James have known since Karen's birth that she had retinitis pigmentosa. Karen's maternal grandmother also had this progressive disease as well as her great-grandmother. Karen always said that she was not troubled by the disease because she felt her prognosis was very positive. Both her great-grandmother and grandmother did not become blind until they reached their nineties. Karen frequently commented that by the time she became blind, she wouldn't care because she would be too old to do anything anyway. Every year when Karen would have her yearly or semi-yearly eye exam, the ophthalmologist would caution Karen that her sight was worsening, but Karen did not seem to believe him. Mr. and Mrs. James tried to help Karen come to terms with what was happening; however, they could not make any inroads. They even took her to a psychologist, hoping that this would help her come to terms with whatever lay ahead. Karen stood firm in her refusal to believe that the prognosis for her eye disease would be different from that of her great-grandmother and grandmother. The psychologist told Mr. and Mrs. James that she felt Karen was depressed. Karen denied this. She claims to be a "happy, carefree teen," but her parents think otherwise. Karen also denies losing weight, even though her mother knows that she has lost at least 5 pounds in the past 6 months.

 Case Study Activity

INDIVIDUAL OR GROUP CASE ANALYSIS

Answer the following questions and be prepared to discuss them in class.

1. What is retinitis pigmentosa?

_____

_____

_____

2. Is it reasonable to expect Karen to learn Braille at this point in her schooling? Why or why not?

_____

_____

_____

_____

_____

_____

3. Is it possible that Karen could succeed in her classes without any intervention? Why or why not?

_____

_____

_____

_____

_____

_____

4. Should Karen follow her parents' advice and give up the cheerleading squad? Why do her parents think this is a good idea? What is Karen's perspective?

_____

_____

_____

_____

_____

_____

_____

5. Do you think that Karen's visual impairment negatively influenced her relationship with her boyfriend? Will it change her relationship with her other friends? Why or why not?

_____

_____

_____

_____

_____

_____

_____

6. Does Karen need mobility training? Does the fact that she has been attending this school for the past 3 years, when she had her sight, have anything to do with the amount or type of training she will need?

_____

_____

_____

_____

_____

_____

_____

7. If you were Ms. Ziebert, what would your priorities be in terms of working with Karen? How would you accomplish these objectives?

_____

_____

_____

_____

_____

_____

_____

8. If you were one of Karen's other teachers in the regular education curriculum, how would you help Karen adjust to her new situation?

_____

_____

_____

_____

_____

_____

_____

9. How could Karen's adolescent development be affected by this visual impairment?

_____

_____

_____

_____

_____

_____

_____

Lauren

Lauren is a 13-year-old seventh grader at Woodlawn Middle School who has recently transferred from another state. Although Lauren has an inherited bilateral sensorineural hearing loss in the severe to profound range, she is able to use her voice for communication purposes. Most of her speech is intelligible, and she is also an excellent speech reader. At her previous school, Lauren had a full-time sign language interpreter whom she shared with another deaf adolescent. The situation worked out well because the school system placed both of the girls in the same classes with the interpreter. Lauren's other school was located in a large metropolitan area as compared to Woodlawn Middle School, which is in a rural area.

Lauren is an attractive adolescent, who is also a very bright and caring individual. She was well thought of at her other school, and although she has only been at Woodlawn for a few weeks, it appears that she has made

a good adjustment. She is also doing well academically. Her English teacher was so impressed by her first paper that she encouraged her to join the staff of the school newspaper as a reporter. Lauren has received Bs on all of her geometry quizzes and a B+ on her first civics test. She works with the speech therapist for 30 minutes twice a week and has access to the learning lab when she needs help with her assignments.

When Lauren's parents, Mr. and Mrs. Baylor, who are both deaf, came to school for the IEP meeting, they were provided an interpreter because neither of them speak. During that conference, school personnel reviewed the previous goals and discussed Lauren's educational goals. During the discussion the parents asked why Lauren's sign language interpreter was not present at the IEP meeting. It was at this point that the pupil assessment team informed the parents that Lauren would not have an interpreter at Woodlawn

Middle School. When the team evaluated Lauren, they concluded that she had the capability to achieve without an interpreter because of her strong speech reading and oral language ability. Mr. and Mrs. Baylor were very distraught. They insisted that in order for Lauren to be able to achieve according to her full potential, she would require the services of an interpreter. Lauren interjected at this point, saying that she was doing fine and things were different here because she was the only deaf student in the school, and it wouldn't make any sense for her to have an interpreter all to herself. Mr. Baylor quickly signed a message to Lauren that surprised her as well as the interpreter. It was obvious that Lauren was going to be in big trouble when she got home. Lauren didn't say anything more for the rest of the meeting. The Baylors refused to sign the IEP. It is their position that Lauren would be a straight-A student with the help of an interpreter. They will not consider her educational program to be appropriate if she makes only Bs and Cs, which they are certain will happen if she does not get the help she needs.

Background Information:

Mr. and Mrs. Baylor are both congenitally deaf. Neither of them had a pleasant school experience. Mrs. Baylor's school experience was dismal until she convinced her parents that she should go to the state residential school for children with hearing impairments. Mr. Baylor struggled through the public school system until he was 15 and then dropped out. He was the object of considerable ridicule by many of his hearing classmates. Because he was never able to use his voice for communication purposes, he was socially isolated from his peers. He also felt that his teachers always considered him to be less intellectually able because he was deaf. It was Mr. Baylor's dream to become a lawyer, but he soon realized that he would never have the educational opportunities to fulfill that dream. Mr. Baylor became very successful as a businessman later on in life, but he has never forgotten his painful school experiences. He is determined that his daughter will be given the educational opportunities that he missed.

 ## Case Study Activity

INDIVIDUAL OR GROUP ACTIVITY

Answer the following questions and be prepared to discuss them in class.

1. What is a bilateral sensorineural hearing loss? Do most individuals who are congenitally deaf with a severe to profound loss learn to speak intelligibly?

_____

_____

_____

_____

_____

_____

_____

_____

_____

_____

2. Does Lauren have a legal right to a full-time interpreter? Since her previous school district provided her with this service, does this mean that Woodlawn must do the same? How can services differ from state to state or city to city? What laws might influence this case?

_____

_____

_____

_____

_____

_____

_____

3. Do you think that Lauren should be given a full-time interpreter? Explain your answer.

_____

_____

_____

_____

_____

_____

_____

4. How could the school work with Mr. and Mrs. Baylor to resolve this difference of opinion regarding Lauren's needs?

_____

_____

_____

_____

_____

_____

_____

5. Have this family's past experiences influenced their perception of Lauren's educational needs? Why or why not?

_____

_____

_____

_____

_____

_____

_____

6. What will happen if the Baylors refuse to sign the IEP?

_____

_____

_____

_____

_____

_____

_____

Markell

Markell is a 12-year-old student in the sixth grade at Harris-Crown Middle School. He was born with retinal dysplasia, a condition that has resulted in blindness. For the past 3 years he has been attending a state residential school for children with visual and hearing impairments. This year he is being mainstreamed into Harris-Crown. He is attending all regular classes with the exception of 1 hour per day when he is attending a resource program. Mrs. Padilla, Markell's special education teacher, has been consulting with Markell's regular education teachers to help with this transition. Things are not going as well as Mrs. Padilla had hoped. Markell hasn't made any friends yet, and his teachers are less than enthusiastic about his presence in their classes. Markell has only been in school for 6 weeks now, and many of his teachers are complaining about his behavior. Three of these teachers have asked Mrs.

Padilla to keep Markell with her for longer periods of time instead of sending him to their classes.

Mr. Milford, Markell's science teacher, has vociferously complained about Markell's inattentiveness in class. Mr. Milford says that Markell's attention span is so short that he seems more like a first or second grader than a sixth grader. It is very disturbing to Mr. Milford that Markell is constantly pressing, rubbing, and pushing at his eyes instead of paying attention to the lecture. When Markell is not "playing with his eyes," he's rocking back and forth while he's shaking his head up and down. It does not appear to Mr. Milford that Markell is getting anything out of his science class. He hasn't given Markell an exam yet, but he has told Mrs. Padilla that he doesn't expect much from this student. He has also told Mrs. Padilla that he is not going to be able to comply with her request to give her his exams a week in advance, so that Mrs. Padilla can Braille them for Markell to take with the rest of the class. Mr. Milford said that he just can't prepare exams that far in advance.

Mrs. Gagnon, Markell's English teacher, is also expressing frustration with this student. She has complained to Mrs. Padilla that he has yet to turn in any of the three assignments that she has requested since school started. These assignments have all been writing assignments. Mrs. Gagnon knows that Markell has been given two books on tape to listen to as a requirement for the papers that are to be written. She also knows that Markell has not even finished one of these books, and she doesn't understand why he can't keep up with the rest of the class given that he has been provided with these modifications. Mrs. Gagnon is also bothered by the fact that Markell acts like he's "really out of it" in class. He never seems to be listening to any of the other students' responses, and when Mrs. Gagnon asks him a question, he never looks at her when he's responding.

Markell's math teacher, Mr. Jensen, thinks that this student should be in the special education classroom for the entire day. He certainly doesn't think that Markell should be in his math class. He has explained to Mrs. Padilla that math has to be taught with the chalkboard or transparencies. Mr. Jensen does not believe that a student who cannot see the visual explanation of the problem-solving strategies has a place in this class. "It's a waste of the kid's time, and it's a waste of my time," said Mr. Jensen.

Background Information:

Markell was the tenth child born to a single mother who was in her twenties. Markell's mother, Ms. Girod, had a seventh-grade education when she started her family. Since then, her family has lived a precarious existence with the help of friends and relatives. For the most part, family life for Markell has been chaotic. In addition to Ms. Girod's limited education, she also struggles with a significant drinking problem. From a very young age, the older children in the family were left, not only to fend for themselves, but also to care for younger siblings. The family has been separated on many occasions when social services found evidence of neglect and placed the children in foster care. Usually when this would happen, Ms. Girod's extended family would step in and try to help her get her children back by providing a place for the family to live. Ms. Girod would stop drinking long enough to get her children back, but once they were with her again, she would resume her pattern of alcohol abuse and child neglect. The last time the children were taken from her, social services had a very difficult time placing Markell because of his visual impairment. It was decided that he should attend the state residential school because a suitable home environment could not be found for him.

Last year, Ms. Girod once again managed to get the support of her extended family to help her find a small house so that she could get her children back from various foster and group home situations. There are six children living in this new home as Ms. Girod has had two more children since social services took her other children away. Of the original 10 children, six are now old enough to have found other living arrangements. Markell and his three teenage brothers are living with his preschool brother and sister.

 ## Case Study Activity

INDIVIDUAL OR GROUP CASE ANALYSIS

Answer the following questions and be prepared to discuss them in class.

1. Why do you think that Markell is rubbing his eyes? If you were his teacher, would this behavior bother you? If so, what would you do about it?

_____

_____

_____

_____

_____

_____

_____

_____

_____

2. Mr. Milford is suggesting that Markell's distracting behaviors, such as rocking in his seat and shaking his head, are related to a short attention span. Could there be another explanation?

_____

_____

_____

_____

_____

_____

_____

3. Is it reasonable for Mrs. Gagnon to expect Markell to finish his assignments in the same time allowed for students who do not have visual impairments? Why or why not?

_____

_____

_____

_____

_____

_____

_____

4. Why do you think that Markell never looks at the person who is speaking? Do you think that it would be a reasonable goal to encourage him to respond to the speaking by looking in that general direction? Why or why not?

_____

_____

_____

_____

_____

_____

_____

5. What do you think of Mr. Jensen's perception of the way math should be taught? Should Markell be provided with his math instruction in the special education classroom, or should Mr. Jensen adapt his instruction so that Markell can learn in his classroom?

_____

_____

_____

_____

_____

_____

6. How can Mrs. Padilla work with each of these three teachers to help them provide modifications for this student? Write a summary of the modifications each teacher needs to make.

Mr. Milford, science

_____

_____

_____

_____

_____

_____

_____

_____

Mrs. Gagnon, English

_____

_____

_____

_____

_____

_____

_____

_____

_____

Mr. Jensen, math

_____

_____

_____

_____

_____

_____

_____

_____

_____

_____

7. Do you think that Markell's behaviors are interfering with his socialization at Harris-Crown? Do you think these behaviors have anything to do with Markell's background? Explain your response.

_____

_____

_____

_____

_____

_____

_____

8. Do you think that Markell would be more comfortable and experience more success at the residential school he was attending? Why or why not?

_____

_____

_____

_____

_____

_____

_____

_____

Ted

Ted is a 6-year-old kindergarten student in Mrs. Montoya's classroom. Ted has been blind since shortly after his birth due to retinopathy of prematurity. He did not attend preschool, so he does not have any structured school experience. Mrs. Montoya has never had a student with a visual impairment in her class. She really wants Ted to have a successful year, and she believes that it will be good for her other kindergarten students to have Ted as their peer. Ted is scheduled to spend the entire day in the classroom. For 30 minutes per day, he will have the services of a special education teacher, Mr. MacManus, who will be teaching Braille and mobility to Ted. For the rest of the day, Mrs. Montoya has been told that Ted will be learning the same curriculum as the other kindergartners. Mrs. Montoya has also been informed that increasing Ted's socialization with his peers has been specified as an important IEP goal for this beginning school year. Development of different types of listening skills—such as attentive, analytical, appreciative, and selective listening—has also been identified as an important preacademic goal.

Ted is a shy child with a charming personality. He is a healthy child, but he gives the appearance of being fragile because he is small for his age and pale compared to the other children. Mrs. Montoya was immediately won over by his sweet disposition and sense of humor. She carefully positioned his desk in the middle of the classroom surrounded by students whom she knew would provide assistance until Ted could navigate the classroom independently. During the first week, she developed a plan whereby Ted would have a friend assigned to him every day for recess and lunch. This friend would help Ted get used to the playground, cafeteria, and restroom. Since all the kindergartners are assigned a classroom chore, she assigned Ted the chore of picking up books in the reading corner and reshelving them.

When Ted's mother, Mrs. Shields, heard about Mrs. Montoya's plans for increasing socialization, she was less than enthusiastic. Mrs. Shields told Mrs. Montoya that she did not want Ted to be on the playground without the direct supervision of an adult. She further told her that without that type of supervision, she was afraid that Ted would be hit by a swing or a baseball or would be involved in some other playground accident. Mrs. Shields was also upset when she discovered that her son's desk was in the middle of the room instead of being next to the teacher's. And she also didn't like the idea of assigning Ted a classroom chore, saying, "It should be obvious that my son can't do all of the things the other students are expected to do—he should be getting more help for his school work instead of cleaning up the room." Mrs. Shields told Mrs. Montoya that if she didn't feel that she had the time to provide Ted with more help and supervision, that she would request another kindergarten classroom where the teacher could.

Background Information:

Mr. and Mrs. Shields are both professionals, and Ted is their only child. When he was born 10 weeks premature, they were in a state of shock. They felt ill-prepared to deal with the numerous medical problems confronting their son. Mrs. Shields quit her job and began devoting herself full time to her son's recovery. When they were told that Ted would be blind, Mrs. Shields had to be medicated for an anxiety disorder. With time, the Shields were able to accept Ted's disability and became dedicated to fulfilling his needs. Mrs. Shields did not send him to preschool because she was afraid he would be hurt on the playground, or the teacher would have no idea how to work with him. Instead Mrs. Shields began researching visual impairments and provided him with a preschool curriculum in the home environment. She considered home schooling Ted instead of sending him to public kindergarten, but Mr. Shields was against it. He feels that Ted is lonely and needs peer interaction. Mrs. Shields would prefer that this socialization take place later when Ted is physically larger and less fragile. Ted's father argues that he is a normal child who only looks fragile because he spends all of his time indoors and doesn't get the exercise he needs. Ted's pediatrician agrees.

 Case Study Activity

INDIVIDUAL OR GROUP CASE ANALYSIS

Answer the following questions and be prepared to discuss them in class.

1. What do you think about Mrs. Montoya's beginning plans for Ted's socialization? Will these place Ted in dangerous situations? If you were Ted's teacher, how would you facilitate socialization?

2. If you were Ted's parents, what recommendations would you give to Mrs. Montoya for Ted's socialization?

3. Should a child like Ted be home schooled until he is more physically fit and less likely to be injured at school? Why or why not?

_____

_____

_____

_____

4. Why is Ted learning Braille? Are there any other methods he could be learning to use instead of Braille? Will Mrs. Montoya be expected to learn Braille?

_____

_____

_____

_____

_____

_____

5. How will Mrs. Montoya teach the different types of listening skills to Ted? Why is it important to differentiate various types of listening for Ted?

_____

_____

_____

_____

_____

_____

6. What will Mr. MacManus be teaching Ted with regard to mobility? What strategies might he use? What might be some of the objectives he sets for Ted?

_____

_____

_____

_____

_____

_____

_____

_____

7. How can Mrs. Montoya and Mrs. Shields reach a compromise that will benefit Ted?

_____

_____

_____

_____

_____

_____

_____

Valerie

Valerie is a 10-year-old fourth grader at Desert Elementary School. Valerie's family has recently moved to the area from a large city in a neighboring state. At her previous school, Valerie spent most of the instructional day in a resource room where she was provided assistance from a vision specialist. Valerie has been identified as a student with low vision; her right eye is her best eye at 20/180, while her left eye is at 20/200. At Desert Elementary, there are no other students with visual impairments. This school is designated as a full inclusion school, meaning that there are no special education resource or self-contained programs. The principal, Ms. Vanatta, has assured Valerie's mother, Mrs. Kemp, that Valerie will have the services of an itinerant vision specialist, who will be collaborating with her classroom teacher to ensure that appropriate modifications are made for her.

It has been 2 months since Valerie started at Desert Elementary, and she has yet to see her vision teacher. Ms. Vanatta called Mrs. Kemp and told her that there would be a delay in getting services for Valerie because the vision specialist is out on maternity leave, but she would be returning shortly. When Mrs. Kemp objected, she was told that there was only one vision specialist for the county, so nothing could be done until she came back to work. When Mrs. Kemp asked if Valerie could get help from an occupational therapist as she

did in her previous school, Ms. Vanatta told her that would not be possible until they held Valerie's IEP meeting which, of course, couldn't occur until the vision teacher was back at school. Mrs. Kemp didn't want to cause trouble in Valerie's new school, so she decided not to say anything more.

Meanwhile, it seemed that Valerie was becoming very unhappy. She was complaining of terrible headaches when she came home from school each day. She told her mother that she hated her new school, and that she didn't have any friends. Valerie also told Mrs. Kemp that she didn't want to go to physical education class ever again because the teacher was so mean to her. Mrs. Kemp decided that she had better go to the school and find out what was going on.

She made an appointment to meet with Mrs. Ames, Valerie's fourth-grade teacher. When she arrived for the conference, she couldn't help but notice that Valerie's desk was at the back of the classroom. She told Mrs. Ames that Valerie had to have her desk in the front row. Mrs. Ames replied that she used a rotation system for moving the desks around in the classroom so that every student would have the opportunity to sit in the front row. She further told Mrs. Kemp that she didn't need to worry about Valerie because she was one of the brightest students in the class, and it didn't seem to matter where she sat, most of her work was excellent. There were a few areas of concern that Mrs. Ames did address. Although Valeria was considered to be a straight-A student in most subject areas, Mrs. Ames stated that she would most likely be getting a D in penmanship because of illegible handwriting. Mrs. Ames expressed concern that Valerie wasn't socializing well with her peers. She also mentioned that Valerie had difficulty staying in her seat; she was frequently out of her desk, moving around the room when she was supposed to be working. When Mrs. Kemp asked Mrs. Ames if she were aware that Valerie had a significant vision problem, Mrs. Ames said that she did notice that Valerie was "cross-eyed and she had a habit of flicking her eyes that was distracting." By this point, Mrs. Kemp was starting to get angry. She tried to explain that Valerie was almost legally blind and that the distracting eye "flicking" that Mrs. Ames described was an involuntary eye movement referred to as nystagmus. Mrs. Ames replied that she had a hard time believing that Valerie had a vision problem when she didn't even wear glasses. Mrs. Kemp continued to discuss Valerie's vision needs, but she had the distinct impression that Mrs. Ames wasn't really listening. Mrs. Ames told her that she had to end the conference because she had a doctor's appointment for which she couldn't be late. In parting, she told Mrs. Kemp that she shouldn't worry about Valerie's academics; instead, she should spend her efforts helping her daughter make new friends. Mrs. Ames suggested that a soccer team might be just the thing for Valerie.

Mrs. Kemp had intended to visit the physical education teacher, but Mrs. Ames advised against it. She said, "Let me give you some advice. Mr. Ledbetter runs a pretty tight ship, and he doesn't take kindly to parents telling him how to teach his classes. If you want your daughter to have a chance in his class, you had better let the two of them work out their own problems." Mrs. Kemp is now extremely angry and upset, but she's not sure what to do. She's wondering what her next step should be. She's starting to think she should call her brother, who is an attorney.

Background Information:

Valerie was involved in a car accident when she was 3 weeks old. Her mother had taken her out of the car seat to feed her just before the accident occurred. Valerie sustained a head injury, but the doctors were unsure about the effects. To this day, the doctors do not know whether Valerie's vision problems occurred as a result of the accident or whether she was born with an eye defect. She has had numerous operations for the strabismus, but Valerie's eyes are still not aligned. The nystagmus developed shortly after 6 months of age. From Valerie's preschool years, numerous types of lenses have been prescribed for her, but they have all caused her to have severe headaches and have not helped with her vision. She needs enlarged print, which she then reads from a near point of approximately 4 inches distance.

Visual–motor difficulties were present from the beginning. When Valerie was an infant, she couldn't perform such activities as transferring a rattle from her left to her right hand. Her occupational therapist referred to Valerie's problems in this area as being the result of a major "sensory integration deficit." She couldn't throw a ball until the second grade. Valerie still cannot hop on one foot or skip, nor has she ever learned to ride a bike or roller-skate. At her previous school, Valerie had occupational therapy on a daily basis and adaptive physical education. Her IEP goals for these areas were extensive.

Valerie has always had a difficult time with socialization. Because of her vision problems, she can't recognize faces until the individual is standing within a foot of her. But through the years, Valerie did make some good friends, many of whom were her classmates in the gifted program at her previous school. It took a long time to establish these friendships, but they were lasting relationships. Several of her old friends still call and write to Valerie. It saddens Mrs. Kemp to see Valerie struggle to make new friends at Desert Elementary.

 ## Case Study Activities

PART I:
ROLE PLAYING

Break into groups of five and assume one of the following roles: Mrs. Kemp, Mr. Henslow (Mrs. Kemp's brother), Mrs. Ames, Ms. Vanatta, and Mr. Ledbetter. Simulate a meeting in which the group attempts to resolve this problem. Following the activity, write a summary of the resolution.

Resolution

_____

_____

_____

_____

_____

_____

_____

_____

_____

_____

_____

_____

PART II:
INDIVIDUAL CASE ANALYSIS

Assume the role of a parent advocate and explain in a written narrative how you would assist Mrs. Kemp in solving this school problem. Included in this narrative should be: (a) an identification of the major problems, (b) a list of possible solutions, and (c) recommendations for the implementation of those solutions. Your response should be approximately two pages in length.

PART III:
INDIVIDUAL OR GROUP CASE ANALYSIS

Answer the following questions and be prepared to discuss them in class.

1. Is it legal for the principal to say that Valerie will not have any services until her vision teacher comes back from maternity leave? What laws might influence this particular situation? What should have been done in this situation?

_____

_____

_____

_____

_____

_____

_____

2. Why do you think that Valerie is having so many headaches?

_____

_____

_____

_____

_____

_____

_____

_____

3. If Valerie had friends at her previous school, why is she having problems making friends at Desert Elementary? What strategies could Mrs. Ames use to facilitate her socialization at her new school?

_____

_____

_____

_____

_____

_____

_____

_____

4. Why do you think that Valerie has such a difficult time with visual–motor activities?

_____

_____

_____

_____

_____

_____

_____

_____

_____

5. What do you think is happening in the physical education class? What kinds of adaptations should be made for Valerie?

_____

_____

_____

_____

_____

_____

_____

6. What could be a plausible explanation for why Valerie is moving around Mrs. Ames' classroom? Since Valerie is doing so well in school, is it possible that Mrs. Ames is right, and that she doesn't require any modifications? Explain your response.

_____

_____

_____

_____

_____

_____

_____

7. What is the distinction between low vision and blindness? What do the terms strabismus and nystagmus refer to?

_____

_____

_____

_____

_____

_____

8. If you were Mrs. Ames, what general strategies would you implement in the fourth-grade classroom to assist this student?

_____

_____

_____

_____

_____

_____

_____

_____

_____

Gifted and Talented Needs

CHAPTER 9

Arletha

Arletha is a 10-year-old fifth grader at Walters Elementary School. Her language arts teacher, Mrs. Abrams, is impressed with Arletha's ability to write short stories and plays. Mrs. Abrams was initially surprised when Arletha turned in her first couple of stories, because Arletha is not one of her better students. In fact, her grades are generally in the low C to high D range. It is Mrs. Abrams' opinion that Arletha's literary works are of such a high quality that she could benefit from the gifted program. However, when she referred Arletha for the gifted program, she was informed by Mrs. Obe, the program's teacher, that Arletha did not qualify. Mrs. Obe told Mrs. Abrams that Arletha's scores on the *Stanford Achievement Test* (1990) were reviewed and that she was also given the standard screening test, the *Raven's Progressive Matrices* (Raven, Court, & Raven, 1986), for admission into the program. Arletha's achievement scores ranged from the 15th percentile in math to the 50th in reading comprehension. Her composite score on the *Raven's* was at the 25th percentile. Mrs. Obe made it clear to Mrs. Abrams that Arletha's scores were well below that which is required for entrance into the school district's gifted and talented program.

Mrs. Abrams accepted Mrs. Obe's assessment of Arletha and became resigned to the fact that she must have been wrong about Arletha's talent. Two months later, Arletha turned in a notebook of haiku poetry for an assignment. Mrs. Abrams was astounded at the brilliance of Arletha's work. She took the notebook to Mrs. Obe's room and asked her to review Arletha's poetry and reconsider Arletha for the gifted and talented program at Walters. Mrs. Obe casually glanced through the poems and replied that they were nice, but irrelevant. According to school district standards, only achievement scores and the results of the *Raven's* could be considered. Mrs. Abrams then asked her if that type of measurement were a fair assessment for an African American child like Arletha. Mrs. Obe laughed and said, "Well, she's an American, isn't she? Of course, it's fair, especially the *Raven's*, which requires only puzzle-solving skills without language. It's one of the most culture fair tests there is."

Background Information:

Arletha lives with a foster family. It is the fourth foster family with which she has lived since social services took her away from her parents who are crack addicts. As soon as Arletha entered a Headstart preschool at the age of 3, her teachers started filling out reports regarding neglect. These continued for 3 years until social services took Arletha and her brothers and placed them in different foster homes. Arletha was sexually abused by her first foster family when she was in first grade. Her second foster family kept her for 3 months, then the mother found out she was pregnant and became too tired to care for her. The next foster family abruptly left the state after caring for her for 8 months. Before Arletha was placed with the fourth foster family, social services evaluated her as being a depressed child who was in need of counseling. However, no one followed up on that recommendation.

Case Study Activity

INDIVIDUAL OR GROUP CASE ANALYSIS

Answer the following questions and be prepared to discuss them in class.

1. How is it possible that Arletha's achievement scores are so low, yet her creative writing is exceptional? Does this mean that the achievement test is invalid? Why or why not?

_____

_____

_____

_____

_____

_____

_____

2. Do you agree with Mrs. Obe's remarks about the fairness of the tests that are used for screening for the gifted and talented program? Are certain tests more culture fair than others? Why or why not? Describe the *Raven's Progressive Matrices.*

_____

_____

_____

_____

_____

_____

_____

3. Do you think Arletha is gifted? Why or why not?

_____

_____

_____

_____

4. Should Mrs. Abrams persist in trying to get Arletha into the gifted program, or should she try to adjust her own instructional program to better meet her needs? Explain your response.

5. Describe how Mrs. Abrams could modify the curriculum so that Arletha could fulfill her potential in creative writing. Give five possible strategies.

6. Should the fact that Arletha is an African American child have anything to do with her assessment for the gifted and talented program? Are there any other factors in this case that should be considered in assessing this child's potential? Explain your answer.

_____

_____

_____

_____

_____

7. Do you think that entrance requirements to gifted and talented programs should be so high that the program is reserved for a select few who can best benefit from it, or should requirements be flexible enough to consider many different variables that affect a child's performance? Support your answer.

_____

_____

_____

_____

_____

_____

_____

_____

_____

Jeffrey

Jeffrey is an 8-year-old child in the fourth grade at Fosterville Elementary School. Since his mother, Ms. Cates, recognized him as functioning well above his preschool peers, she asked the school district to waive the requirement that states all children must be 5 years of age by September 15th in order to begin kindergarten. She wanted Jeffrey to start school even though he would not be 5 until October 10th. The school district refused to do this, so Jeffrey had to wait another year to start school. As soon as Jeffrey started kindergarten, his teacher recognized that his abilities were well above that of the other children. He was tested during his kindergarten year and determined to be a "highly gifted" child. Since Fosterville did not have a gifted program suitable for meeting Jeffrey's needs, the school decided to allow him to skip both first and second grades in an effort to provide him with a more intellectually stimulating environment. His teachers agreed that he probably should have skipped third grade also, but they felt that his social needs would go

unmet if he progressed that rapidly through the school years.

Ms. Cates felt that Jeffrey went through third grade in a state of complete boredom. She thought that his enrichment program was also a waste of time. The teacher for this program would meet with the children once a week and assign them a project, supposedly based on their interests. She would then review their progress on this project during enrichment time for the next three weeks until the assignment was due. The enrichment teacher didn't seem to have any interest in Jeffrey's projects, which usually dealt with mechanical engineering, nor did she seem to have any ability to guide him in his ideas. By the time Jeffrey had finished third grade, it appeared to Ms. Cates that he had lost a lot of his interest and enthusiasm for school and learning. His mother is determined that fourth grade will be more stimulating for her son.

When she spoke to Mrs. Lewis, the fourth-grade teacher, at the beginning of the school year, she carefully explained her concerns regarding her son's schooling and the expectations she had for this school year. She felt that Mrs. Lewis largely ignored her concerns and turned the discussion around to focus on Jeffrey's needs for socialization. Mrs. Lewis told her that the third-grade teacher described Jeffrey as a "social isolate," who really had no friends at school. She suggested that this should be an area of focus for Jeffrey's fourth-grade year. Ms. Cates is aware that Jeffrey doesn't have very many friends at school, but Jeffrey explains this by saying he's just not interested in the same things that his peers find interesting.

Mrs. Lewis stated that Jeffrey's third-grade teacher told her that Jeffrey has a morbid interest in tragic events reported in the news. She advised Ms. Cates to keep him away from the television and newspaper when something tragic has transpired as a means of dealing with that behavior. Ms. Cates was aghast at Mrs. Lewis' interpretation of this aspect of Jeffrey's behavior. Jeffrey appears to focus on tragic events because he is more sensitive to issues of ethics, morality, and evil than his peers, who don't fully understand many of these issues at this point in their development. Ms. Cates can't believe that Mrs. Lewis could be so ignorant as to have such an interpretation of Jeffrey's sensitivity. She also can't believe that the third-grade teacher said all these negative things about Jeffrey to Mrs. Lewis, and yet never mentioned anything to her. She found herself getting too emotional to continue the conference.

On the way home, in the car, Ms. Cates started crying and couldn't stop. She feels that Jeffrey doesn't have a chance to get an appropriate education for his needs in that school. She wishes she could send him to the Gates School for the Gifted, a private school which has the best reputation in the city and a yearly tuition bill of $10,000. As a single mother, she's doing all she can to meet the family's basic needs. There's seldom any money left over for anything except an occasional movie or trip to the museum. Sometimes she feels that Jeffrey's intellect is more of a burden than a gift. And today she's feeling like a bad parent because she can't get her son the help he needs from the school system.

Background Information:

Jeffrey's father and mother were never married. They had been engaged for a brief period of time, but the relationship soured when Jeffrey's mother became pregnant. Even though Jeffrey's father lives in a neighboring town, he has never seen him or taken any interest in establishing a relationship with him. Ms. Cates feels responsible for not providing her son with a father, even though she has tried everything she could to continue the relationship. Ms. Cates knows that Jeffrey understands and internalizes this rejection with an understanding well above his age. It makes her feel very sad that such a wonderful child isn't appreciated and loved by both parents. She also feels that if Jeffrey had a "real father," there would be two people to provide for him, making it more plausible for Jeffrey to go to a private school and get the kind of education he needs.

 ## Case Study Activity

INDIVIDUAL OR GROUP CASE ANALYSIS

Answer the following questions and be prepared to discuss them in class.

1. Do you agree with the school district's policy of having a specific birth date requirement for entrance to kindergarten? Should the school district allow exceptions? Do you think that most school districts currently allow exceptions? Explain your answers.

_____

_____

_____

_____

_____

_____

_____

_____

2. Should Jeffrey have skipped third grade also? Why or why not?

_____

_____

_____

_____

_____

_____

_____

_____

3. Was it wrong for Jeffrey's third-grade teacher to share her concerns about Jeffrey's social behavior with the fourth-grade teacher, but not with Ms. Cates? Explain your answer.

_____

_____

_____

_____

_____

_____

_____

4. In your opinion, does Jeffrey have a socialization problem that should be addressed? Why or why not? Should socialization be the primary area of focus for Jeffrey in the fourth grade?

_____

_____

_____

_____

_____

_____

_____

_____

5. Do you agree with Ms. Cates that Jeffrey's giftedness causes him to be more sensitive about ethics and morality? What does the literature on giftedness suggest about this topic?

_____

_____

_____

_____

_____

_____

_____

_____

6. Do you think Jeffrey's enrichment program in the third grade was appropriate for his needs? In what ways could it have been modified to be more relevant for Jeffrey?

_____

_____

_____

_____

_____

_____

_____

7. If you were Ms. Cates, what would you do to provide an appropriate education for your son, given your circumstances?

_____

_____

_____

_____

_____

_____

_____

_____

8. Do you think it is more or less stressful to parent a gifted child than to parent a more typical child? Explain your response.

_____

_____

_____

_____

_____

_____

_____

_____

_____

Jenna

Jenna is a 13-year-old student in the seventh grade at Newman Middle School. She has been in the gifted and talented program since she was in the fourth grade. At the time of admission to that program, her IQ was determined to be 140. Jenna seemed to really enjoy the accelerated academic program during the elementary school years. She had told her teachers that she looked forward to the program at Newman. However, she has recently told her counselor, Mr. Jarwan, that she wants to drop out of the program. Jenna told him that she dislikes it because it's "stupid and boring." Mr. Jarwan is concerned about her lack of interest, but he's even more concerned about her grades.

Since Jenna has started middle school, her grades have been on a steady decline. Her current average is a C–. Mr. Jarwan can't believe that she is doing so poorly when she has always done so well in school. When he has tried to talk with her about her grades, she has generally rebuffed him, saying that she's doing the best she can. Mr. Jarwan can't seem to get any help from Jenna's

teachers, who view her variously as "sullen," "rude," "unmotivated," and "lazy." The issue of Jenna dropping out of the gifted program may soon be a moot one because Newman Middle School has a policy that stipulates that enrollment in the gifted program is based on maintaining at least a C average. It is unlikely that Jenna will continue to meet that criteria considering her current attitude and grades.

Mrs. Huang, the gifted and talented teacher, agrees with Mr. Jarwan that Jenna could benefit from this program. But it is also her opinion that once a student decides he or she wants to drop out of the program, there's very little any teacher can do about it. She has mentioned several times that many gifted teachers consider task commitment to be critical to any measure of success in this type of program, noting that Jenna doesn't have this kind of interest in the gifted curriculum. Mrs. Huang has resigned herself to the fact that she's "lost another one to the throes of mediocrity."

Background Information:

Last year Jenna's father, Mr. Russo, left her mother for his very young and attractive secretary. The event was totally unexpected. Mrs. Russo had never worked outside of the home, but she was a very bright woman with many intellectual pursuits that she encouraged Jenna to model. Jenna has always been aware at some level that Mr. Russo did not have a high regard for the book clubs, poetry readings, opera, and theater that her mother enjoyed, but she felt that her parents had a relatively happy marriage in spite of their different interests. When Mr. Russo left the family, he did so without making adequate financial provisions for Mrs. Russo and Jenna. They had to sell the house and move into a very small apartment. Mr. Russo paid no alimony and only a modest amount of child support for Jenna.

When Mr. Russo failed to contact Jenna after the split, she went to his office to tell him that she forgave him. He was very nervous and uncomfortable, but he agreed to his first visitation with Jenna and set a date and time to pick her up. Jenna was to spend the day with her father and his fiancée. When the appointed time came, however, Jenna's father did not come to pick her up, nor did he call. Jenna tried to call him, but there was no answer. She has not seen her father since that day at the office. Even though it has been over a year since Mr. Russo left, Jenna's mother has not been able to adjust to her new living situation. She spends most days in her bedroom with the curtains drawn, drinking and smoking cigarettes. She doesn't talk much, and she cries often.

 Case Study Activity

INDIVIDUAL OR GROUP CASE ANALYSIS

Answer the following questions and be prepared to discuss them in class.

1. Why do you think that Jenna is no longer interested in the gifted program? What do you think is the reason behind her dropping grades?

_____

_____

_____

_____

_____

_____

_____

_____

2. What is your opinion of the school district's policy regarding the C average requirement for the gifted program? Explain your response.

_____

_____

_____

_____

_____

_____

_____

_____

3. What do you think of Mrs. Huang's attitude that there's nothing she can do about Jenna's behavior and her decision to drop out of the gifted program? Is she being realistic, or is she not fulfilling her responsibilities as a teacher of gifted students?

_____

_____

_____

_____

_____

_____

_____

4. Are there certain aspects of development that have adversely affected Jenna's school performance? Describe several aspects of psychological development during the middle school years that explain why Jenna is feeling the way she is.

_____

_____

_____

_____

_____

_____

_____

6. If you were Mrs. Huang, how might you work with Jenna to help her? Give four specific strategies.

_____

_____

_____

_____

_____

_____

_____

_____

7. If you were Mr. Jarwan, how might you try to assist Jenna with her problems?

_____

_____

_____

_____

_____

_____

_____

_____

8. What do you think is the prognosis for Jenna?

_____

_____

_____

_____

_____

_____

_____

_____

9. Should Mr. Jarwan and Mrs. Huang attempt to work with Jenna's family? What strategies could they use to establish communication with both parents? How might this coordination of efforts benefit Jenna?

_____

_____

_____

_____

_____

_____

_____

_____

Leo

Leo is a 15-year-old student at Carlton High School. He has been in the gifted program since he was in kindergarten, when his IQ was determined to be 165. He has completed all requirements for graduation and has taken his college boards—he scored in the 99th percentile on both the SAT and ACT. Leo desperately wants to go to college next year, but his parents, Mr. and Mrs. Demchak, have refused to agree to this plan. He has been accepted into the medical biomechanics program of a prestigious university located in New York. He has also been offered a full scholarship by this university. Mr. and Mrs. Demchak have stated that they think their son is too immature to go off to school by himself. They seem to understand that Leo is a highly creative individual, but they don't appear to trust him.

Leo's teachers believe that he should go to college next year. Mr. Gifford, Leo's chemistry teacher, has strongly advocated for Leo's early admission into college. He believes that this student has the potential to make a major contribution to medical science. Mrs. Robbins, Leo's guidance counselor, agrees. As an alumnus of the university that has offered the scholarship, Mrs. Robbins believes that this school is the best possible choice for Leo. When they have talked to Mr. and Mrs. Demchak regarding this recommendation, they feel their opinions have been totally disregarded. It doesn't appear that the Demchaks had their son's best interests in mind when they made their decision against early graduation. Leo's teachers have mentioned the problem of Leo having finished all the courses that were suitable for him through a curriculum compacting approach to instruction. The Demchaks responded, however, that they consider it to be the school's responsibility to provide him with whatever instruction he needs at whatever level is appropriate for his ability.

Background Information:

Leo has always been regarded as a highly creative thinker. His kindergarten teacher told his parents that she had never worked with a child who came up with so many interesting ideas and projects. When he was tested for the gifted program, the evaluation report indicated that Leo possessed "high levels of fluid ability." Other teachers have noted in their reports that his giftedness is characterized by a "quickness in thinking, intuition, and perception." Leo's academic record and teacher reports have always been exemplary.

Mr. and Mrs. Demchak understand, just as well as the teachers, how bright their son is, but they also feel he is too immature to go away to college, especially to a university in such a big city. They have a difficult time teaching him responsibility at home. It's hard for them to imagine what he would do away from home. Not too long ago, Leo got into trouble for vandalizing the community swimming pool. Last week, he came home drunk from a party. A couple of days ago, his mother found several marijuana cigarettes in his dresser drawer. And yesterday, his father caught him trying to crack the security code for the phone company on his computer. These are just a few examples of the problem behaviors that Leo has demonstrated since he started high school. Mr. and Mrs. Demchak understand that it is typical for adolescents to get in some trouble, and they are not overly concerned about these behaviors. However, they believe these behaviors indicate that Leo is not mature enough to live in an unsupervised setting. Mr. and Mrs. Demchak do not want to tell Leo's teachers about these incidents because they think this information may prejudice them against Leo. They want his teachers to continue to think of him in a very positive light.

Case Study Activities

PART I:
ROLE PLAYING

Break into groups of four or five and assume one of the following roles: Mr. Demchak, Leo, Mr. Gifford, Mrs. Robbins, and Mrs. Demchak (an optional role). Simulate a conference in which the participants attempt to resolve this problem. Following the activity, write a summary of the resolution.

Resolution

_____

_____

_____

_____

_____

_____

_____

PART II:
INDIVIDUAL OR GROUP CASE ANALYSIS

Answer the following questions and be prepared to discuss them in class.

1. Do you think Leo's parents should let him accept the scholarship and go away to New York next year? Why or why not?

_____

_____

_____

_____

_____

_____

_____

_____

2. Leo managed to complete all of the high school graduation requirements in 2 years because of "curriculum compacting." Describe this strategy.

_____

_____

_____
_____
_____
_____
_____
_____
_____

3. Is there any relationship between Leo's problem behaviors and his intellectual profile? Explain your position.

_____
_____
_____
_____
_____
_____
_____
_____
_____
_____
_____

4. Should Mr. and Mrs. Demchak tell Leo's teachers about his behavior problems? Why or why not?

_____
_____
_____
_____
_____
_____
_____
_____
_____
_____

5. Should Mr. and Mrs. Demchak be seeking outside help for Leo's problems, or are these fairly normal behaviors that will probably diminish on their own if the Demchaks communicate their disapproval to their son on a regular basis? Explain your response.

_____

_____

_____

_____

_____

_____

_____

6. If Leo stays at Carlton for the next 2 years, how can the school and his teachers accommodate his giftedness and provide him with an education that is motivating and challenging?

_____

_____

_____

_____

_____

_____

_____

_____

_____

Lily

Lily is a 5-year-old kindergarten student at Kincaid Elementary School. She has been in school for only 2 weeks now, and she's having considerable difficulty adjusting. Lily is a very precocious child who is already reading on the second-grade level. She also demonstrates unusual abilities in the areas of art and problem solving. Her parents, Mr. and Mrs. Herrera, do not believe the school is providing her with the education she needs. Lily's teachers feel that all children need to learn basic rules regarding following directions and observing classroom procedures, regardless of whatever strengths they may also possess.

Ms. Gravier, Lily's art teacher, was initially delighted to have a student with such a high level of artistic ability in her class; however, she soon changed her mind. Lily never seemed to be interested in the art projects that Ms. Gravier had developed for the kindergartners. For example, if the art project of the day had to do with line drawings, it was Ms. Gravier's expectation that all of the children would engage in line drawing activity. She did not tell them what to draw, she would merely specify the medium. According to Ms. Gravier, that type of assignment should allow for all students to express themselves as they saw fit.

Frequently, Lily did not want to use the medium that Ms. Gravier had selected. She would refuse to participate and, in a petulant manner say, "I don't feel like markers today. I want to use watercolors." At first Ms. Gravier tried to gently cajole her into completing the project of the day, but as Lily grew more resolute, Ms. Gravier became angry. She finally decided that if Lily refused to complete the specified project, she would sit in the corner and do nothing. Ms. Gravier felt that this was an appropriate consequence for the behavior in question.

Lily's kindergarten teacher, Mrs. Carson, is having problems with Lily as well. She simply will not follow the directions that are given in class or observe the basic classroom rules. For example, when Mrs. Carson starts the day, she has an opening time. At the end of this opening time, she explains the first instructional activity, which is also written on the schedule on the board. As soon as Mrs. Carson starts explaining what the students will be doing, Lily jumps up from the circle and begins the project. She has read the project on the board and figured out what to do, so she wants to start. Mrs. Carson will not allow her to start until all the children have the instructions. While Mrs. Carson is explaining the lesson to the other children, Lily sits there impatiently waiting, muttering things like, "This is stupid. Why do I have to wait?" As a consequence of this behavior, Mrs. Carson frequently makes Lily wait until everyone else has left the circle before she can begin. Sometimes, Mrs. Carson tells her to wait until 5 minutes after everyone else has started the project before she can begin. Lily is responsible for watching the clock so that she will know when she can start.

Another problem is that Lily won't raise her hand to answer questions, and she won't wait until Mrs. Carson gets the entire question out before answering. This is very annoying to Mrs. Carson, because none of the other children ever get a chance to listen to the question and try to figure out the answer. Lily also fails

to stop working when Mrs. Carson tells the students to finish up and start another project. When Lily wants to continue on a project, she flatly tells Mrs. Carson that she is not going to stop until she's done. Mrs. Carson punishes her by withdrawing such privileges as free time or recess. Lily usually ends up crying. She doesn't really care about missing recess, but she does care that Mrs. Carson makes her spend the whole time sitting in her desk, studying spelling words that she knew when she was 4 years old.

Mr. and Mrs. Herrera are furious with the teachers and the principal. They are appalled that there are no gifted programs available until the third grade in this school district. They have asked the principal, Mr. Evans, to intervene. His suggestion is that they should pull Lily out for the year and start her again next year when she is more mature. Mrs. Carson thinks that Lily should be referred for a special education evaluation for behavioral problems.

Background Information:

Lily is the only child of Mr. and Mrs. Herrera, both of whom are doctors. Lily's precociousness has been a source of extreme pride for this family. They will readily admit that they have indulged her, perhaps a little more than they should, because they believe that she needs more flexibility because of her brightness. When she was tested at the age of three, her *Wechsler Preschool and Primary Scale of Intelligence* (WPPSI; Wechsler, 1967) Full Scale IQ was 145. At approximately the same time, they started her in an exclusive preschool. Lily had quite a few adjustment problems in this setting. Her teacher felt that she was prone to temper tantrums, and that she was a very willful child. Finally, after numerous meetings with the school to try to resolve their differences, the Herreras decided to make a large donation to the school's computer lab. There were few problems thereafter.

 Case Study Activities

PART I:
ROLE PLAYING

Break into groups of five and assume the following roles: Mr. Herrera, Mrs. Herrera, Mrs. Carson, Ms. Gravier, and Mr. Evans. Simulate a conference in which the family and the school staff discuss how to resolve this problem. Following the activity, write a summary of the resulting resolution.

Resolution

_____

_____

_____

_____

_____

_____

_____

**PART II:
INDIVIDUAL OR GROUP CASE ANALYSIS**

Answer the following questions and be prepared to discuss them in class.

1. Should Lily be referred for a special education evaluation for her behavior? Why or why not?

_____

_____

_____

_____

_____

_____

_____

_____

2. Should Lily be pulled out of kindergarten and started again next year? Why or why not?

_____

_____

_____

_____

_____

_____

_____

_____

3. Do schools legally have to meet the educational needs of gifted children. Explain your response. Why do you think that the district does not have any gifted programs for children who are in the primary grades?

_____

_____

_____

_____

_____

_____

_____

_____

4. If you were Mrs. Carson, how would you work with Lily to accommodate her learning needs and decrease her behavioral problems?

_____

_____

_____

_____

_____

_____

_____

_____

5. Is it an appropriate strategy for Ms. Gravier to exclude Lily from art activities if she refuses to do what the rest of the class is doing? Why or why not? If you were Ms. Gravier, how would you work with this child?

_____

_____

_____

_____

_____

_____

_____

_____

_____

6. What strategies could the Herreras use to help Lily adjust to the demands of the school environment?

_____

_____

_____

_____

_____

_____

_____

_____

Marcus

Marcus is an 11-year-old fifth grader at McCurd Elementary School. Marcus' teacher, Mrs. Edberg, referred him for testing for the gifted and talented program. Mrs. Edberg believes that Marcus has unusual strengths in the areas of science and math. Mr. Vigil, coordinator of the gifted and talented program at McCurd, told Mrs. Edberg that he reviewed Marcus' cumulative folder and did not find any evidence of achievement high enough to gain entry into the accelerated program. Mrs. Edberg, however, was insistent that Marcus be tested. She genuinely feels that the type of questions he asks during science class is well above the level of any fifth grader she has ever known. Reluctantly, Mr. Vigil agreed to schedule Marcus for an intelligence test that the district uses to identify giftedness.

The psychologist who tested Marcus used the _System of Multicultural Pluralistic Assessment_ (SOMPA; Mercer & Lewis, 1978) to supplement the IQ testing, because Marcus is an African American child. With this system of assessment, Marcus' estimated learning potential (ELP) is determined to be 125, which is approximately 1½ standard deviations above the norm. Since the district policy is to identify all children at 125 or above as gifted, the psychologist has recom-

mended that he be provided access to this program. Mr. Vigil is amazed at this recommendation. He is even more confused when the psychologist tells him that Marcus' IQ would not qualify him for the gifted program if the multicultural assessment procedure had not been used. The psychologist explained to Mr. Vigil that the pluralist assessment technique is a means of taking cultural factors into consideration with standardized testing. In Mr. Vigil's mind, a person is either gifted or not. He can't see that culture has anything to do with a person's IQ.

Mrs. Edberg is gratified when she hears that Marcus will have access to the resources in the gifted and talented curriculum. She is very pleased that the psychologist used a testing procedure that took Marcus' cultural background into consideration. Mr. Vigil is angry. In putting together a placement folder for Marcus, he has discovered that Marcus' reading level is below grade placement; in fact, he is reading almost 6 months below grade level. He calls the district coordinator for gifted and talented programs to complain that the psychologist has recommended the accelerated program for a child who is reading below grade level by using some "multicultural hocus-pocus testing."

Background Information:

Marcus' mother, Ms. Howe, was 14 years old when he was born. His father never acknowledged paternity. Marcus and his mother lived with her family for the first year of Marcus' life. They lived in a small apartment in the projects, which they shared with 12 other relatives, until Marcus' grandmother was caught in the crossfire of a robbery and died of a bullet wound. From that time on, Marcus and his mother moved from place to place, without anywhere to call their home. Ms. Howe and her son were frequently without adequate food and shelter. When Marcus entered kindergarten, his teacher found him to be functioning well below expectancy in all areas of readiness. She referred him for special education testing because she suspected him of being mentally retarded, but he did not qualify for any services. As Marcus' mother has matured, she has struggled to make a better life for herself and Marcus. With the help of welfare, Ms. Howe now has an apartment, which she shares with her sister and two children. She attends a vocational school and is training to be a nurse's aide.

 ## Case Study Activity

INDIVIDUAL OR GROUP CASE ANALYSIS

Answer the following questions and be prepared to discuss them in class.

1. Is Marcus a gifted child? Why or why not?

_____

_____

_____

_____

_____

_____

_____

_____

2. Explain the psychologist's perspective. What is multicultural assessment, and why was it used for Marcus' evaluation? Describe the SOMPA procedure.

_____

_____

_____

_____

_____

_____

3. Explain Mr. Vigil's perspective. Why does he consider multicultural assessment to be "hocus-pocus"?

4. Should a child who is not able to read on grade level be staffed into a gifted program? Would this type of placement have a negative or positive impact on the child? How would the other students in the gifted program react to a peer who was performing well below their achievement level? Would this be an issue?

5. Should Marcus' background be considered in his assessment? Would Marcus' IQ and reading achievement have been higher if he had had a more stable environment during the first 5 years of his life? Could you compare this child's potential to another child who has not experienced the effects of deprivation? Explain your answer.

_____

_____

_____

_____

_____

_____

6. What do you think the district coordinator will do in this case? What would you do if you were the coordinator? Explain why you would make this decision.

_____

_____

_____

_____

_____

_____

_____

_____

_____

_____

7. How could the school work with this family to help Marcus achieve his potential?

_____

_____

_____

_____

_____

_____

_____

_____

_____

_____

8. How could Mrs. Edberg modify the fifth-grade science curriculum to provide a more stimulating learning experience for Marcus? Give four strategies.

_____

_____

_____

_____

_____

_____

_____

_____

Margo

Margo is a 14-year-old freshman at Peninsula High School. She was identified as gifted at the age of 8. The school district provided an excellent program of enrichment, allowing Margo the opportunity to pursue many interests. Margo is accomplished in many areas. She plays first flute with the school band, and she has won many prizes for both her ice skating and dance. Academically, she is above most of her peers in all areas, but she shows the greatest potential in science and math. Her hobbies include poetry writing and painting. Margo has a tremendous amount of energy and has been able to enjoy all of these activities in the past without experiencing stress. This year appears to be different.

Since she has started high school, Margo has begun to feel pressure from her parents, teachers, and friends regarding the amount of time she should be spending on certain activities. The school year started 3 weeks ago, and already Margo has been asked to make certain commitments that would preclude other activities that she has previously enjoyed. For example, her father has told her that he wants the science fair to be her number one priority for this school year. Her speech teacher has asked her to represent the school on a team for Odyssey of the Mind (OM), and her band teacher has asked her to compete as a soloist as well as a member of a trio for the state band contest. Her ice skating coach expects her to train for a minimum of 2 hours per day so that she has a chance at the Metro Ice Competition in the spring, and her dance teacher expects her to be involved in four dance numbers at spring recital as well as performing at numerous other fundraisers during the year.

Because Margo genuinely enjoys all of her activities, she has not chosen to drop out of any of them. However, she has also not been able to arrange her schedule so that she can keep up with all the obligations to which she has committed herself. Margo is starting to miss certain obligations, causing her coaches, peers, parents, and teachers to become angry with her. For example, Margo was half an hour late for dance rehearsal because her band teacher kept the trio late to discuss the upcoming competition. At the end of rehearsal, Margo's dance teacher had a stern talk with her about tardiness. This talk lasted so long that Margo would have been 30 minutes late for OM, but it didn't matter because she was crying too hard to go. By the time she had walked home, there was an angry message on the machine from a peer whom she considered to be a good friend. The message said something to the effect that if Margo didn't take her commitment to OM seriously, then she should drop out and give her part to someone more deserving and more willing to put the time into the team commitment.

Margo started crying again. When her mother came home, Margo told her about some of the pressure she was starting to feel this year. Mrs. Finister, Margo's mother, takes great pride in her daughter's accomplishments. She was very responsive to Margo's emotional state, but she offered no solution, only the encouragement that, "You can do it, sweetie, if you really put your mind to it." Margo continued to feel badly so when her father came home, she tried to talk to him. He immediately offered her what he thought was a realistic solution. He told her to drop everything except the science fair—which is the activity in which Margo has the least interest of all. Mrs. Finister overheard the discussion and came rushing in from the kitchen to castigate Mr. Finister. "Just because you have limited interests, you should not try to force your daughter into the same restrictive mold!" she chastised. Her parents then embarked on a heated discussion as Margo slipped away, feeling that her presence wasn't needed.

The next morning, Margo's OM coach, Mrs. Bricker, caught her as she was coming through the school door. Mrs. Bricker started to reprimand her when she noticed that Margo was going to cry. Margo didn't look very good this morning. She hadn't slept well, worrying that she had let her friends and teachers down and not knowing what to do to make things better. Margo and Mrs. Bricker went into her classroom where Margo tearfully explained how she was feeling.

Later, in the faculty lounge, Mrs. Bricker mentioned Margo's dilemma to a couple of other teachers. She was saying that she really had a lot of empathy for gifted children like Margo because they experienced quite a bit of stress associated with their multipotentiality. Several teachers overheard Mrs. Bricker's conversation and started making negative comments. One of these teachers sarcastically said, "Those poor kids, they have such a rough go of it—good at everything, what a miserable life!" Another teacher remarked, "The only ones who whine and complain more than the gifted kids are their parents." A third teacher emphatically confirmed, "Boy, isn't that the truth."

Background Information:

During her daughter's preschool years, Margo's mother keenly observed Margo's special skills in a wide variety of areas. As a conscientious mother, Mrs. Finister went out of her way to make sure that Margo had the opportunities to explore her many talents. Mrs. Finister watched with amazement as Margo excelled in activity after activity. She never forced Margo into any activity. She didn't have to—Margo seemed to relish every opportunity to learn a new skill or activity. Occasionally Mrs. Finister would think that Margo was involved with too many different activities. Then again, she also felt that Margo was so gifted that it was her responsibility to expose her to as many possibilities as she could, and then let her decide what she wanted to continue later on in life. Mrs. Finister eventually got Margo involved in so many activities that she had to quit her job so that Margo could enjoy full participation. But the truth of the matter is that Mrs. Finister didn't mind because she believed that her most important job was parenting Margo, and she felt fortunate to have a daughter who was so talented.

 Case Study Activity

INDIVIDUAL OR GROUP CASE ANALYSIS

Answer the following questions and be prepared to discuss them in class.

1. If you were Mrs. Bricker, how would you advise Margo? Do you think her parents would agree with this advice? Why or why not?

_____

_____

_____

_____

_____

_____

_____

2. Is it unusual for a gifted student to experience talent in such a wide range of different areas? Margo didn't seem to have any problems keeping up with all her activities in elementary and middle school. Why is she experiencing problems in high school? Explain your answer.

_____

_____

_____

_____

_____

_____

_____

3. What is your opinion of Mrs. Finister's attitude about Margo's activities? What do you think of Mr. Finister's attitude? If you were Margo's parent, how would you counsel her?

_____

_____

_____

_____

_____

_____

_____

4. Do you think that Margo is simply overreacting to her peer's comments about missing OM rehearsal, or do you think that she is experiencing significant stress? What might happen if Margo and her family do not resolve this problem?

_____

_____

_____

_____

_____

_____

5. Why do you think those teachers in the faculty lounge had negative reactions to Mrs. Bricker's comments about Margo? Do you think that many teachers hold those perceptions of gifted students? What do you think is the public's perception of gifted students? Do you think these perceptions influence funding for gifted programs? Explain your answers.

_____

_____

_____

_____

_____

_____

_____

6. Why do you think the teachers in the faculty lounge made negative comments about the parents of gifted students? Is there a stereotype that they may be referring to in this situation? Do you think that parents of gifted children experience increased parenting stress? Why or why not?

_____

_____

_____

_____

_____

_____

_____

7. Do you think that the federal government provides funding for gifted students in the same way that it supports the education of children with disabilities? Why or why not?

_____

_____

_____

_____

_____

_____

_____

_____

About the Author

Peggy L. Anderson is a professor in the Division of Education at Metropolitan State College of Denver. She has taught students with moderate needs at the elementary and middle school levels in South Carolina and Florida. Her master's degree is from the Citadel and her doctorate is from the University of Denver. She completed her postdoctoral work with the Department of Pediatrics at Johns Hopkins University. She presently coordinates the special education program for the Division of Education. Her research there has focused on language–learning disabilities, assessment, legal issues, and inclusion.